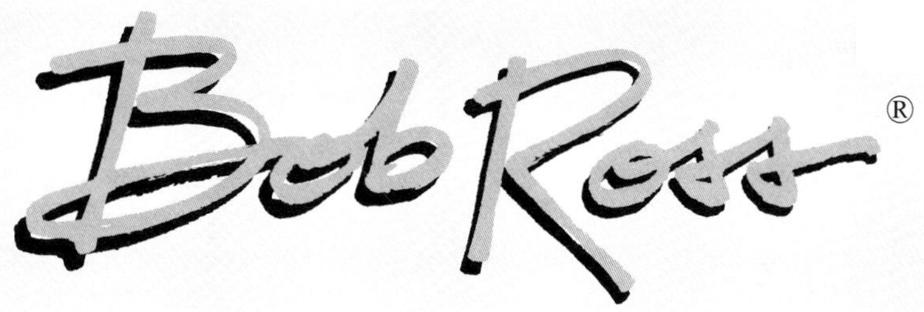

TV's Favorite Artist

P R E S E N T S

Annette Kowalski's

The Joy of Painting® Flowers II

To The Artist

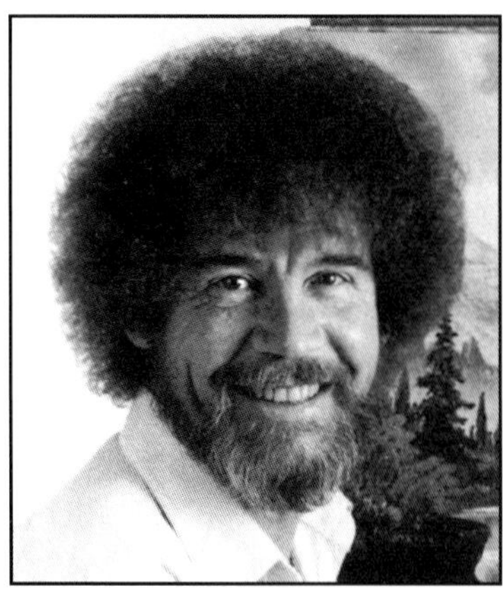

It is with the utmost pleasure and pride that I have the opportunity to present Annette Kowalski and her first Joy of Painting Flowers book. I sincerely believe that with the techniques and equipment she has developed, combined with a little practice, that you will soon be able to complete floral paintings so beautiful that you as well as family and friends will find it hard to believe.

I first met Annette in Clearwater, Florida in 1981, where I was teaching art classes. I was immediately impressed with her warm, caring personality as well as her extra-ordinary artistic abilities. We became instant friends and she and her husband, Walt, began sharing some of their personal history with me.

They had recently lost their oldest son, John, in an automobile accident and their world was shattered. Annette was desperately looking for some type of distraction from her pain and had turned to her love of art as an escape.

As for me, I had recently retired from the United States Air Force and moved from my beloved Alaska determined to share my art with America. This was before my first television show and times were very difficult for an unknown, traveling art instructor.

I spent a week painting with Annette and on several occasions had the opportunity to have dinner with her and her family. They allowed me to share my dreams and goals with them and a bond was formed that lasts to this very day.

On their way home Annette described to Walt the joy felt by herself as well as all of the students that participated in the class. She then suggested they bring me to the Washington, D.C. area where they lived so that their friends could also share in the wonderful painting techniques she had learned.

With this simple beginning the joy of painting was eventually formed and my wife, Jane, and I entered into a partnership with the Kowalskis and the rest is history.

Annette has traveled with me to virtually every corner of the United States and to numerous foreign countries, promoting the television series, teaching classes and spreading the joy of painting. She and Walt have been instrumental in the enormous success enjoyed by our company.

Annette has written and published all of the Joy of Painting books which have opened the world of art to millions of people in every age group and every walk of life. She is also the Executive Producer of the Joy of Painting television series and has worked untold hours to make the show the most popular TV art show in the history of television. And most important, Annette is my best friend.

In this, her first book of her own paintings, Annette shares with you the beauty of floral painting in the same detailed precise manner that we have become so accustomed to in her many Joy of Painting books. She has worked extremely hard to develop a painting technique that ensures success. Use this book as a guide and allow your own imagination and creativity to take you to any world that you desire.

Once again, please allow me to invite you to experience the Joy of Painting Flowers as well as the joy of Annette Kowalski.

Happy Painting,

Bob Ross

1942-1995

This book is dedicated to the memory
of Bob Ross.

Keeping the dream alive.

a.h.k.

Contents

If you are excited by color, then you should be painting flowers. If you are really turned on by a brilliant Pink, a vivid Orange or muted Blues, Lavender and Greens, then you should be painting flowers. Whether painting very realistic flowers or flowers of pure fantasy, I can think of no other subject matter where there are so few color limitations. And color is really what it is all about!

Even if you have never painted before, with just a couple of brushes, several gorgeous colors and a few basic techniques, you will be producing a whole range of exciting flowers. Master just a few basic flower types and you will be able to paint almost any flower; the principals remain the same.

And, if you have been painting for years and years, perhaps using other methods, I think you will find this exciting, new technique will allow you to produce the most exciting, vibrant flowers imaginable.

Having authored and co-authored many, many technical painting books, I have a theory that most people refer to a book, not only to learn a specific technique of painting, but simply hoping to glean new ideas. I think this is wonderful, because if you are only looking for ideas, then you are developing you own special and unique style of painting. I have tried to include many variations and suggestions in this book regarding canvas sizes, backgrounds, colors, types of flowers, etc., and so, hopefully you will view this book as an idea book rather than a "do-it-my-way" book; a reference book to be used by both the beginner and the more advanced painter.

I am very excited about the unique products which have been developed for this technique of flower painting. They, too, have been designed specifically to stimulate your imagination and open up a whole new approach to painting flowers. Never has there been such flexibility as with these products.

This book and these products have been designed to encourage you to create your very own special, unique method of painting flowers, all you need is the desire. However, there are a few rules which must be learned before they can be broken.

As with any technique of painting, the real secret is practice, practice and more practice. Once you have created your own special style of painting, you will truly experience the Joy of Painting Flowers.

HOW TO USE THIS BOOK

A picture is worth a thousand words, they say. So, in this book, we've tried to eliminate so many words and rely more on pictures. I hope you find this helpful. I suggest that before you paint your first floral painting, read the Introduction and study the Basic How-To Photo section of this book to familiarize yourself with the various floral-painting techniques. Each of the paintings in this book has its own inclusive set of how-to photos and instructions, but if at any stage of the painting you feel you need more in-depth instruction, you can refer back to the Basic How-To Photos.

PAINTS

All of the paintings in this book were done with a limited palette of only 14 oil colors. Unlike the landscape paints, Bob Ross Soft Paints have been formulated to a very soft, creamy, smooth-flowing consistency. In order to achieve the pure, brilliant color so desirable in a floral painting, and to avoid "muddy" paintings, this palette does not include earth colors. The number of colors you can mix (including earth tones) from just these fourteen basic colors is almost limitless.

The colors we use are:
Alizarin Crimson*
Ivory Black
Cadmium Orange
Cadmium Red Light
Cadmium Red Medium
Cadmium Yellow Light
Dusty Rose
Flower Pink*
Magenta
Mauve*
Sap Green*
Titanium White
Turquoise
Ultramarine Blue*
*(*Indicates transparent color)*

Because this is a Wet-On-Wet technique, the first step is to make the canvas wet and slippery. For this we use Liquid Opal, which is a special base paint, designed to complement flowers from all three color groups; Red, Blue and Yellow.

Or, you may simply apply a thin, even coat of Oil Paint Medium. Oil Paint Medium can also be used to thin any of the oil colors to a base coat consistency. Both of these are slow-drying, oil-based mediums and should not be confused with the Gessos, which are water-based. Black, White and Gray Gesso are water-based mediums which dry very quickly. They are used to precoat the canvas, enabling you to paint dramatic florals on a dark background, to underpaint various components of a painting (such as baskets and vases) but also simplify or dispense with the application of background color. Gesso should be applied with a foam applicator and never with the pure natural, bristle brushes that we use.

FLORAL BRUSHES

All of the Bob Ross Floral brushes are pure, natural bristle brushes and have been specially designed to work with Bob Ross Soft Oil Colors. They are made of pure, soft but stable bristles. These brushes are very important to this technique of floral painting. I have tried to limit the number of brushes used in this book to basically the Floral 1/2" brush and the Floral filbert brush. As you progress, and begin your own experimentation, you may wish to add the 3/4" brush, the small round brush and the floral fan brush to your collection. The 3/4" brush can be used to apply background mediums and colors or to paint very large flowers. It is especially good for painting large double-wide tapered leaves, such as those in the Iris painting. The small round brush is great for intricate "sketching" and adding important small details. The floral fan brush can be used to blend and soften small areas and individual flower petals.

BOB ROSS LANDSCAPE BRUSHES

The Bob Ross 1" and 2" landscape brushes are also pure, natural bristle brushes and can be used to apply the Liquid Oil Mediums to the canvas and can also be used to apply and blend background colors.

The Bob Ross 2" Soft Blender brush is wonderful for blending out harsh brush strokes, creating very soft, smooth, silky flowers. Beginner painters especially will find this brush helpful.

The Bob Ross #2 Liner brush is used to add small buds, vines, twigs, tendrils, but most importantly, your signature.

CLEANING THE BRUSHES

All of the brushes should be cleaned with Bob Ross Odorless Paint Thinner. AVOID CLEANING ANY OF THESE BRUSHES WITH SOAP AND/OR WATER. Clean the Floral brushes by first removing excess paint with a very soft paper towel, then "swish" the bristles in a smooth-bottomed container of odorless paint thinner until all traces of paint are removed from the bristles. Dry the bristles on a soft paper towel, squeezing them back into shape.

The bristles of the Bob Ross Landscape brushes can be cleaned against a screen in the bottom of a large container of Bob Ross Odorless paint thinner, briskly shaken to remove excess thinner, then thoroughly dried with soft paper towels.

After thorough cleaning, all brushes can finally be restored to their original condition with Bob Ross Brush Conditioner.

CANVAS

The canvas you use is very important. You will need a good quality double-primed canvas that will not absorb the Liquid Base-Coat Mediums, leaving you with a dry surface. (Remember, this is a Wet-On-Wet technique.) For this reason, I do not recommend canvas boards or single-primed canvases. Some people prefer an ultra-smooth canvas; I prefer a canvas with some "tooth" and find that I can economically replace my brushes more frequently with money saved on more expensive, portrait-smooth canvases.

EASEL

A good, sturdy easel is recommended any time you are working with large brushes. Also an easel which holds your canvas upright will allow you to step back periodically from your painting. It is very difficult to critique your painting in its entirety if you try to paint with your canvas on a flat surface.

OTHER SUPPLIES

Palette:

Any non-absorbent palette can be used for this technique of floral painting. The Bob Ross Disposable Floral Palette is recommended but you may prefer the Bob Ross acrylic palette.

Painting Knife:

A small knife for moving and blending paints on your palette is a nice addition. The Bob Ross small knife works great for this purpose.

Foam Applicators:

An inexpensive foam applicator for applying Gesso to your canvas is a must. NEVER use your natural bristle brushes with Gesso.

Wax Paper:

Wax paper, from the grocery store, is a wonderful surface for practicing brush strokes. It is also great for making transparent patterns.

Freezer Paper:

Freezer paper, from the grocery store, is a wonderful, inexpensive source of large-sized paper. The dull side of the paper is good for tracing flower designs and the shiny side can be taped to a firm surface and used as a palette, in a "pinch".

Dressmakers Tracing Paper:

This is the best way I have found to copy a pattern or drawing to the canvas. It is very inexpensive and comes in many colors and does not leave permanent markings on your canvas.

Opaque Projector:

I find an opaque projector an invaluable tool for

painting flowers. Almost all of my paintings ideas are taken from photos I have taken and there is no better way to enlarge and transfer the exact likeness of a flower from a photo to canvas than with an opaque projector. An opaque projector also allows you to enlarge the design to the exact size of the canvas you will be using. I suggest a bottom-loading projector, which gives you the option of projecting the design from an open book.

Paper Towels:

To protect the delicate bristles of your Floral brushes, I recommend the softest, non-shredding paper towels or facial tissues you can find.

BASIC INSTRUCTIONS

Transferring the Design:

I think the best way to begin a painting is with a very loose, free-hand sketch. But, if you would like to begin your painting with a tracing, I have included a line drawing, over a grid, with each project. Simply place an opaque projector over the line drawing and project the design to the size of your canvas. I prefer projecting the design to a large sheet of paper (freezer paper is wonderful for this and is 18" wide!) and tracing it with a felt tip marker. Then transfer the design to the canvas with Dressmakers Tracing Paper. That way, I have a permanent, enlarged copy of the design which can be used over and over. Or, you can use a very thin mixture of Oil Paint Medium and flower color on one of the small Floral brushes to rule your canvas into a 16-square grid. Enlarge the floral design, by copying it, square for square, to your canvas. Don't worry about the grid lines on your canvas, they will disappear when you apply the background colors; or you can just wipe them away with a soft paper towel after your design has been transferred to the canvas.

Loading the Brushes:

1"and 2" Landscape Brushes:

These large brushes, used for base-coating the canvas and backgrounds, are loaded by just dipping into Liquid Opal or Oil Paint Medium. Or, they can be loaded by simply pulling both sides of the bristles through the Soft Oil Color on your palette.

Floral Brushes:

All of the Floral brushes can be loaded to a chiseled edge by first dipping the brush into Oil Paint Medium then pulling both sides of the bristles through the paint color of choice; smoothing the paint into the bristles, forcing them to a sharp, chiseled edge.

Liner Brush:

To load the liner brush, thin the desired paint to ink-like consistency by first dipping the liner brush into Oil Paint Medium. Slowly turn the brush as you pull the bristles through the paint, forcing them to a sharp point.

A WORD ABOUT COLOR MIXING

I think Sap Green is the floral painter's best friend, but is very bright and can rarely be used alone for foliage. Try brush-mixing a very, very small amount of Ultramarine Blue or Alizarin Crimson or Cadmium Red Medium with Sap Green to make a variety of gorgeous foliage colors.

My favorite Brown color is made with a mixture of equal parts of Alizarin Crimson and Sap Green. This is the most incredible color and can be used to paint a wicker basket, a clay pot or copper. It is also wonderful for woody stems and twigs. Once you work with this mixture, you may never want to use tubed Browns again!

HOW TO GET STARTED!

Begin by reading through the entire written instructions and studying the how-to photos for the project you have chosen to familiarize yourself with all of the suggested procedures. If necessary, refer to the Basic How-To Photos and take a few minutes to make a waxed-paper practice sheet of any component of the painting you may feel is necessary. (If you are lucky enough to have a new canvas wrapped in plastic, that plastic covering, before it is removed from the canvas, is also a wonderful place to practice brush strokes, allowing you the bounce of a stretched canvas.)

But there is no substitute for the learning that takes place as you do an actual painting. Don't be afraid of the canvas, it's your friend! If you do make a brush-stroke or flower you don't like, just brush it out and begin again. Very soon, you will be completing your own masterpieces - truly experiencing "the Joy of Painting Flowers". Have fun, it's only paint!

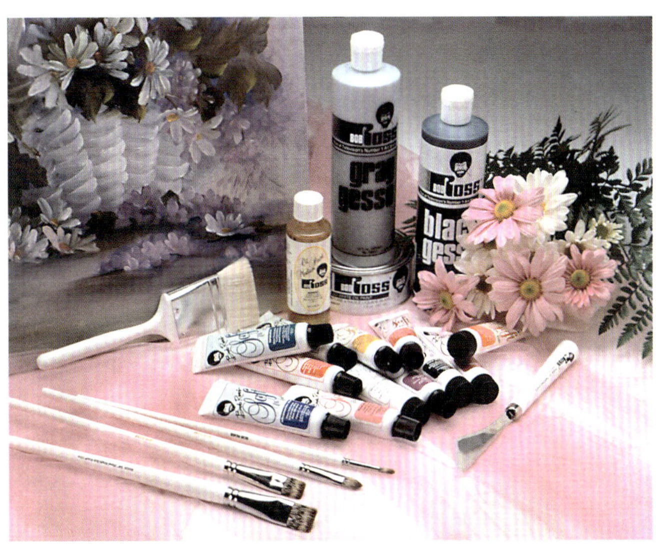

Basic How-To Photographs

How to Paint a Basic Leaf

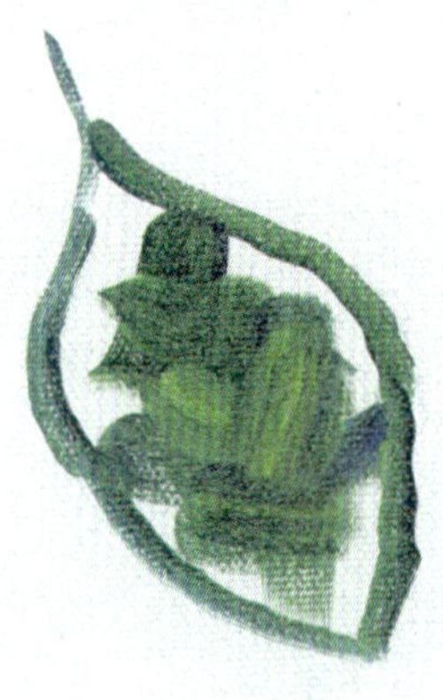

1. Start by using the small round brush and thinned paint to loosely sketch the basic shape of the leaf. Use the 1/2" brush and criss-cross strokes to block in leaf color in the center of the leaf.

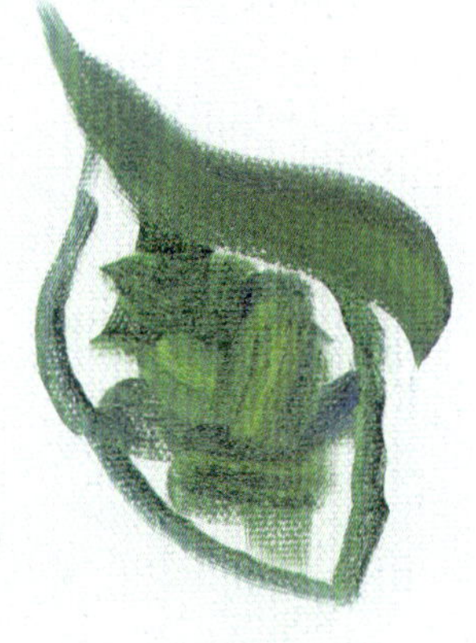

2. Reload the brush to a chiseled edge and angle the first stroke from the outside of the leaf to the base of the leaf.

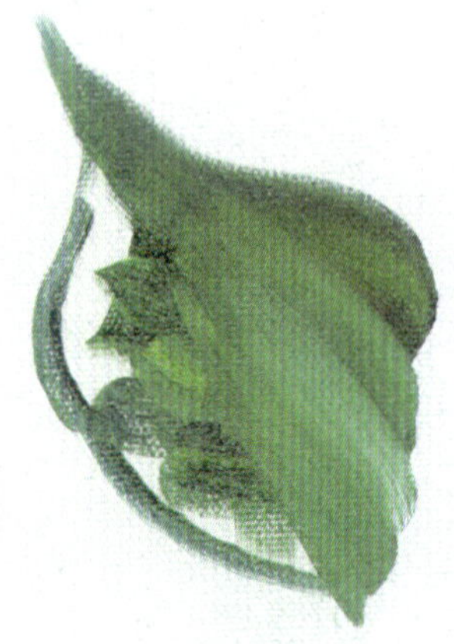

3. continue angling a series of overlapping strokes from the outside edge of the leaf to the center base of the leaf. Complete one side of the leaf...

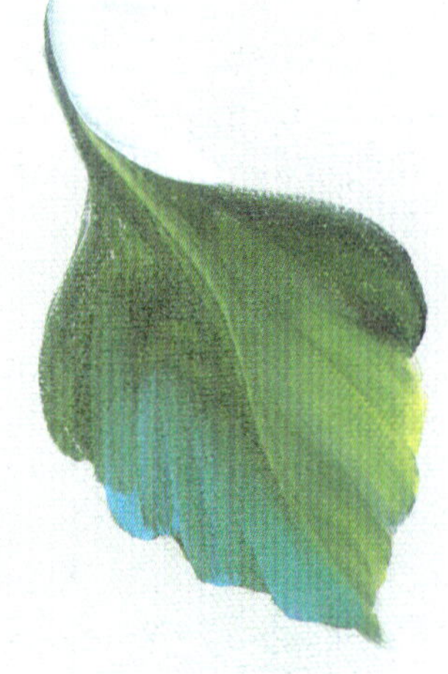

4. ...then repeat for the second side of the leaf. Use the chiseled edge of the brush to 'cut' in the center vein. Highlight the leaf with Yellow; reflected light on the shadowed side of the leaf is Turquoise.

How to Paint a Cluster of Leaves

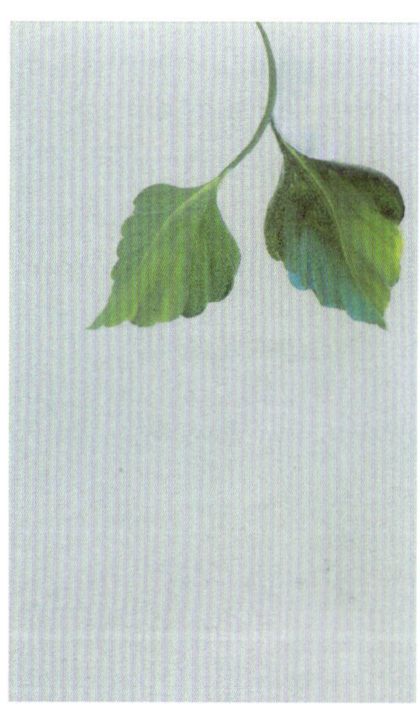

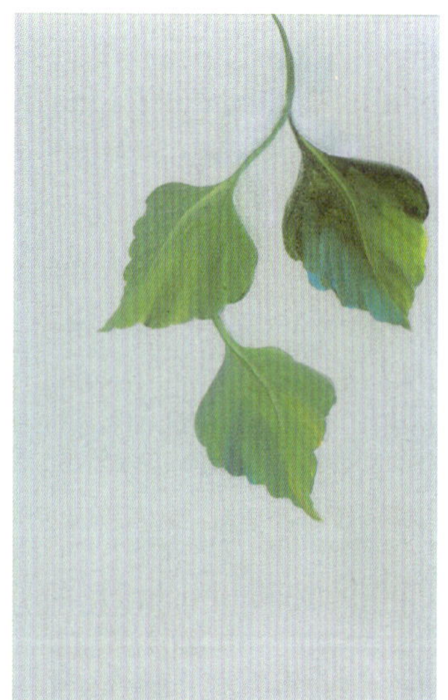

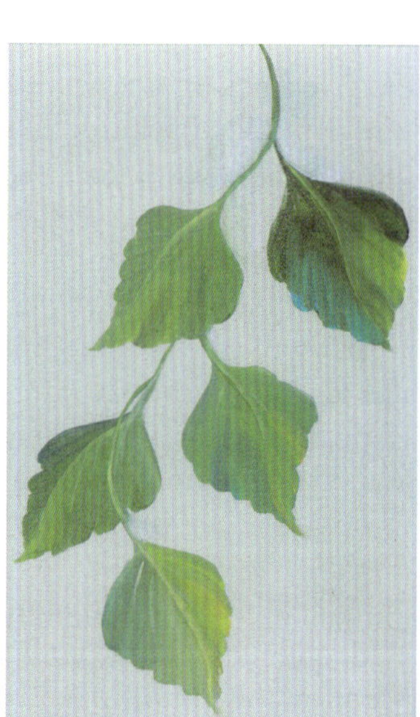

Connect a cluster of leaves with long, flowing stems all painted with the chiseled edge of the brush.

How to Paint a Basic Flower

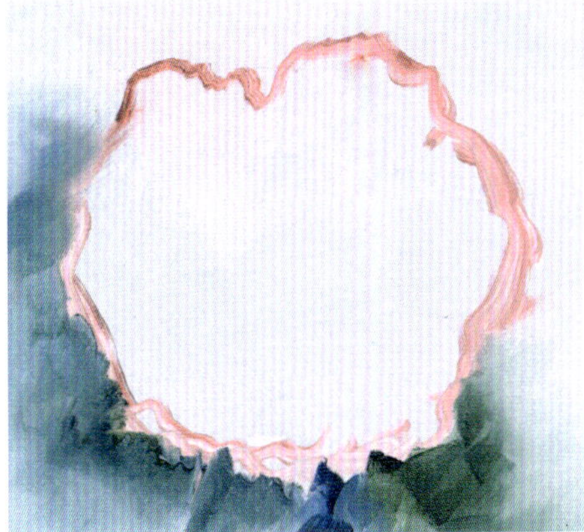

1. Sketch the flower placement and add foliage colors to the background.

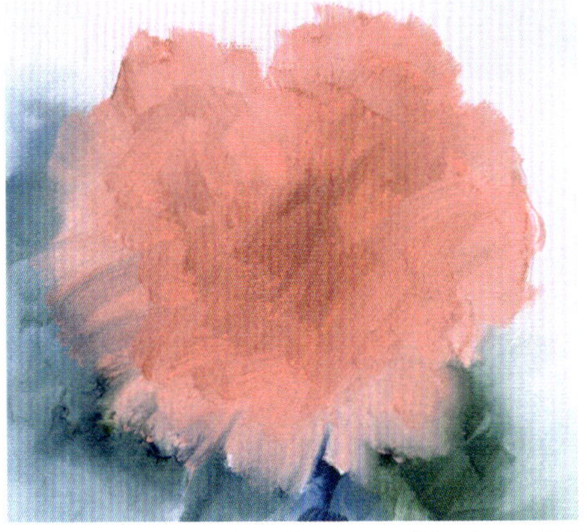

2. Underpaint the flower with the 1/2" brush and a thin mixture of Oil Paint Medium and Alizarin Crimson.

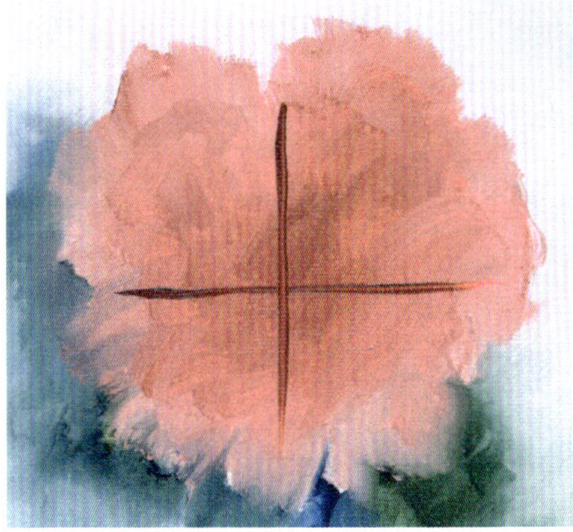

3. Use the 1/2" brush and Alizarin Crimson to divide the flower into four large petals.

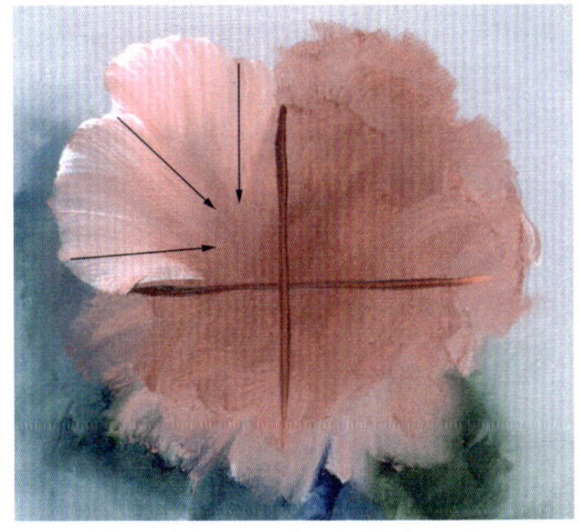

4. With White on the 1/2" brush, start at the outside edge of one large back petal, and direct a series of overlapping strokes towards the center of the flower.

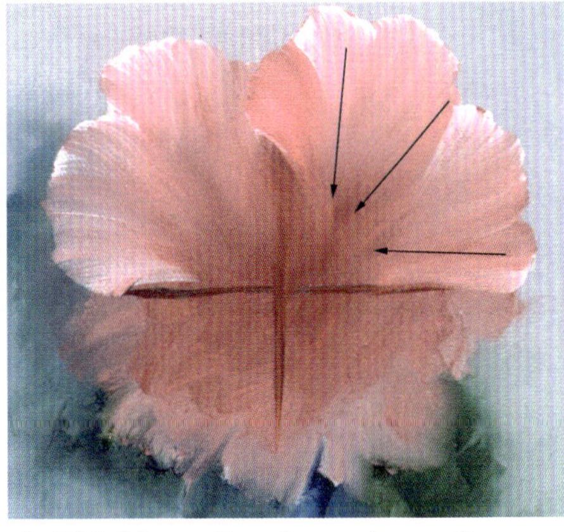

5. Thinking of each petal as a fan shape, add the second large petal, again using White on the 1/2" brush.

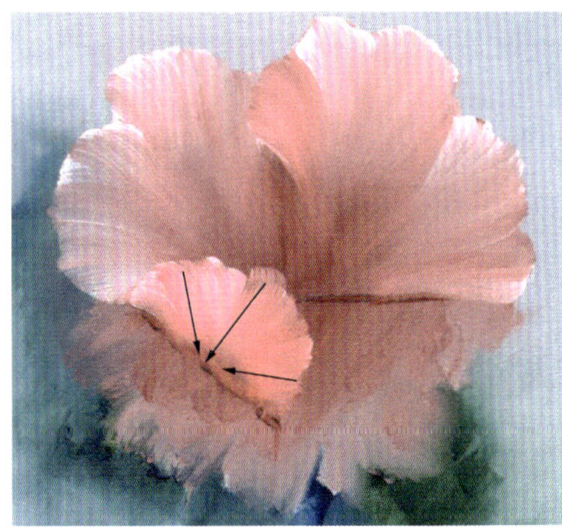

6. "Fold" up the lower front petal with a series of overlapping strokes all directed towards the base of the petal.

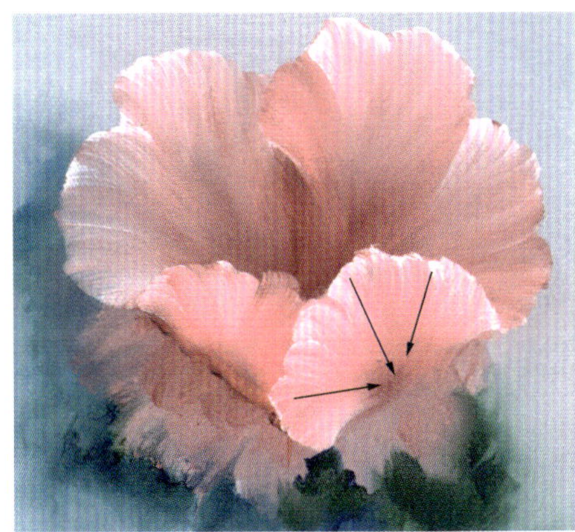

7. Make a series of overlapping strokes to create the second, folded up, fan-shaped petal.

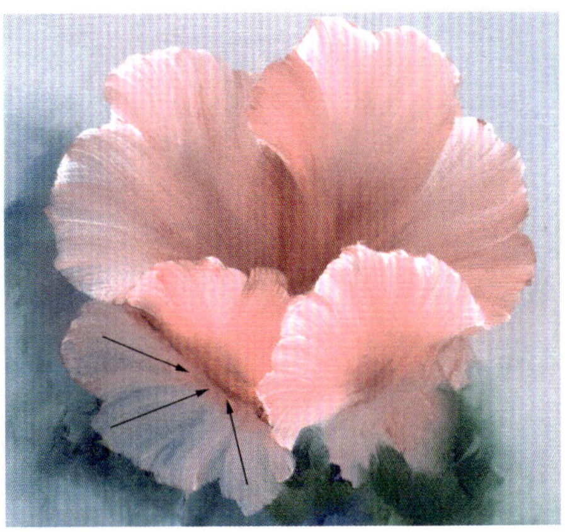

8. With very little White on the brush, add fan-shaped petals at the base of the flower with overlapping strokes ...

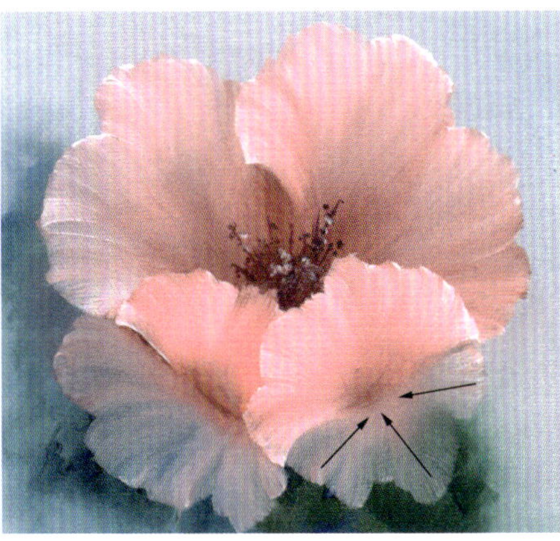

9. ... all directed towards the center of the flower. Add dark stamens and dots of Yellow to the center to complete the flower.

Basic How-To Photographs

How to Paint Tapered Leaves

1. Load the 1/2" or 3/4" brush to a chiseled edge. Start at the base of the leaf with a fine line, or stem...

2. ...turn the brush to its flat side for the entire length of the leaf...

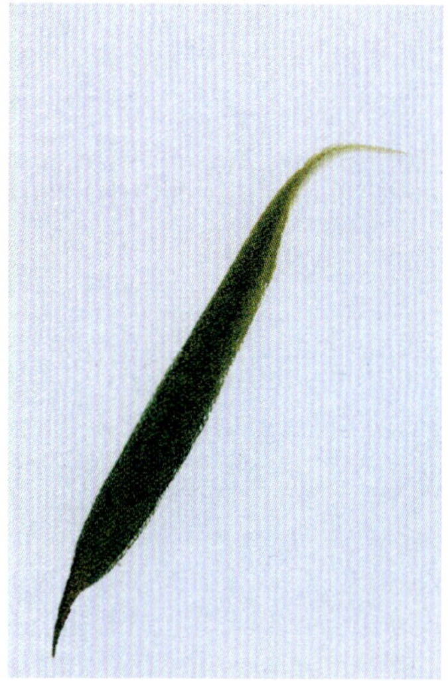

3. ...turn the brush back to its chiseled edge to complete the leaf with a long, thin, tapered tip.

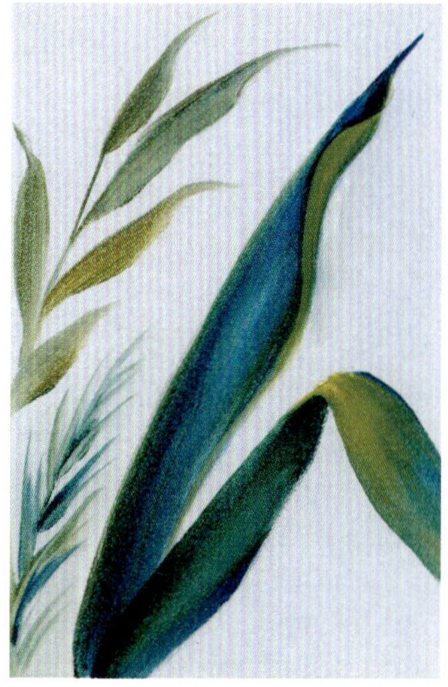

4. You can paint a single tapered leaf or clusters of tapered leaves. Paint large double-wide leaves and tapered leaves that bend and fold.

How to Paint Daisies

1. Load the filbert brush with thinned White. Use the side of the brush to paint two or three curved strokes to indicate the foreshortened petals at the base of the daisy.

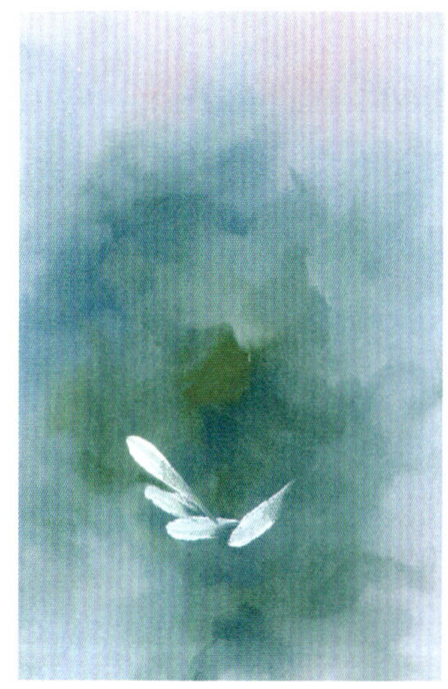

2. To add the back petals, start at the outside edge, apply pressure, then release pressure as you stroke in towards the daisy center.

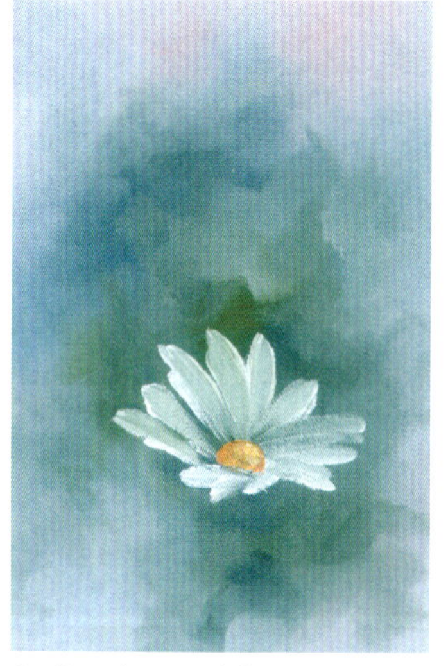

3. Continue adding petals to the desired degree of fullness. To complete the daisy, use a half-round stroke of Orange; highlight with dots of Yellow.

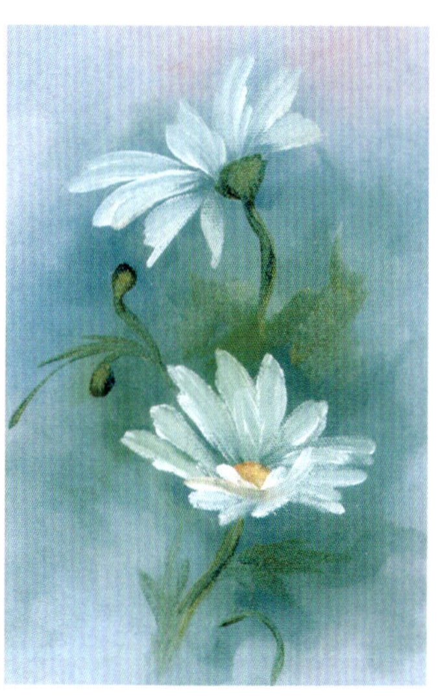

4. Add additional petals, buds, half-opened daisies, stems, leaves and tendrils, if desired.

How to Paint a Clay Pot

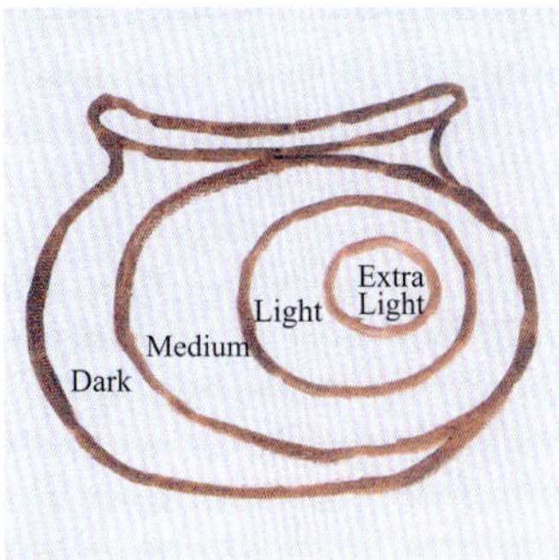

1. Start by loosely sketching a pot and the placement of four values of color.

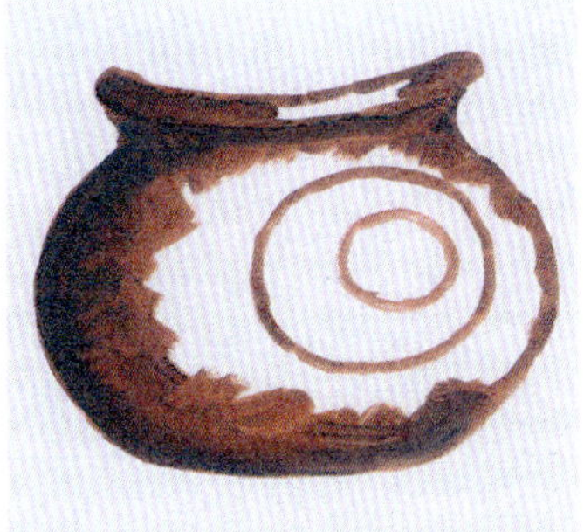

2. Use the 1/2" or 3/4" brush and loose criss-cross strokes to block in the dark value.

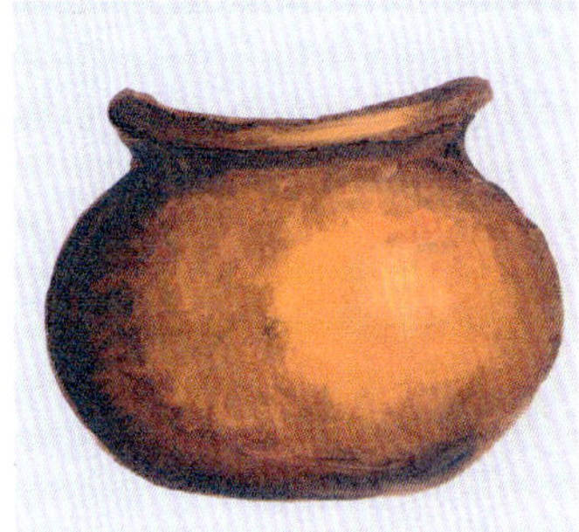

3. Add the middle value, light value and extra light value with loose criss-cross strokes.

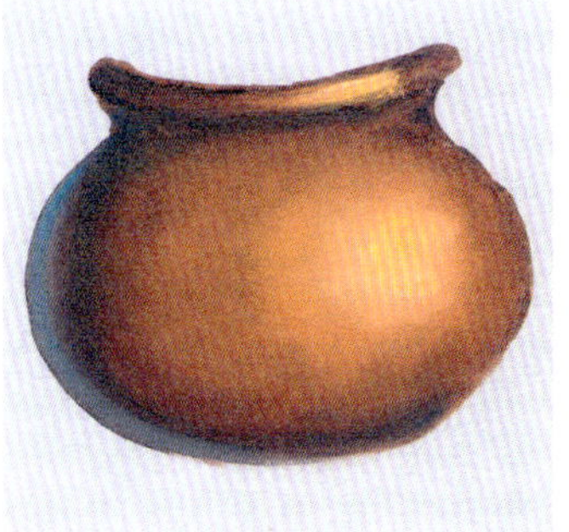

4. With a clean, dry 1/2" or 3/4" brush, use criss-cross strokes to blend and merge the values. Complete the pot with the fan brush and sweeping, horizontal strokes.

How to Paint a Basket

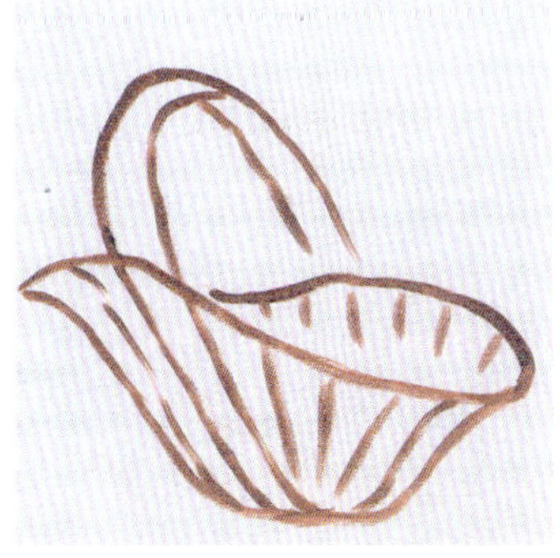

1. Lightly sketch the basket with the small round brush and a thin mixture of Oil Paint Medium and a color of your choice. (For a brown basket, you can use equal parts of Alizarin Crimson and Sap Green.)

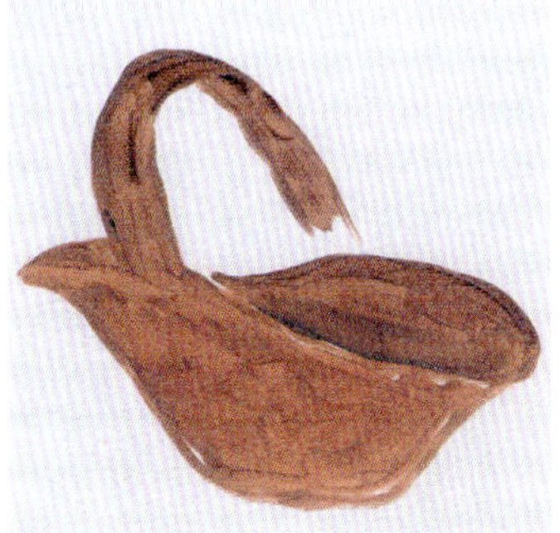

2. Use the 1/2" or 3/4" brush to underpaint the basket with loose criss-cross strokes.

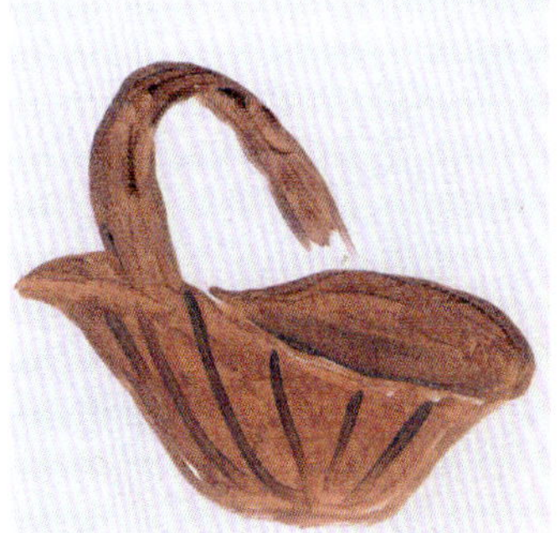

3. With a dark color, add the vertical ribs to the basket. (For the brown basket, add a small amount of Ultramarine Blue to the Alizarin Crimson-Sap Green mixture.)

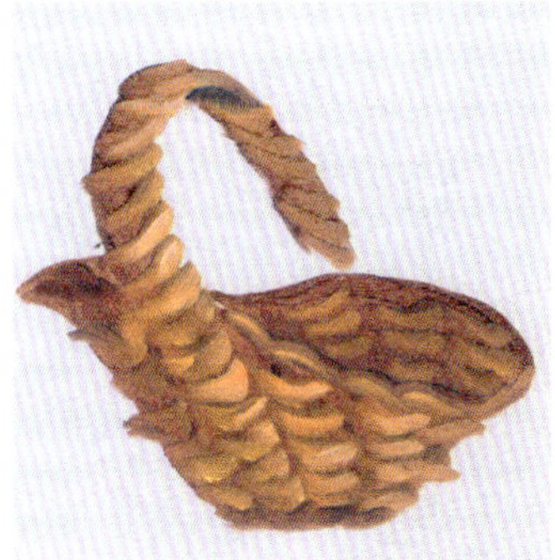

4. Use the filbert brush with a lighter mixture (White and/or Yellow) and a series of curved strokes to 'weave' the basket. Add touches of bright, final highlights with White.

Basic How-To Photographs

How to Paint Cluster Flowers

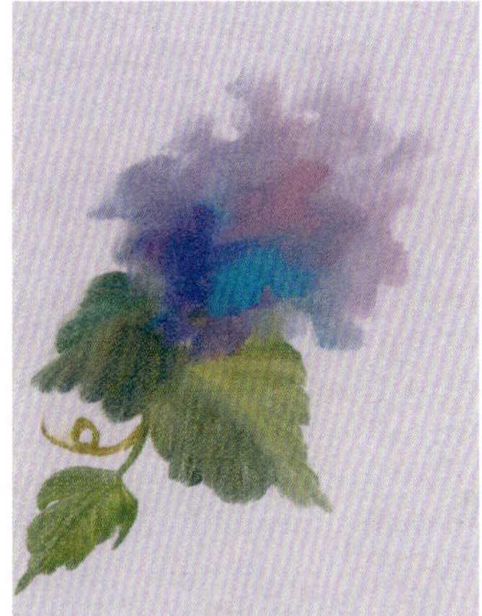

1. Use the 1/2" brush and criss-cross strokes to loosely underpaint the mass of florets with a thin mixture.

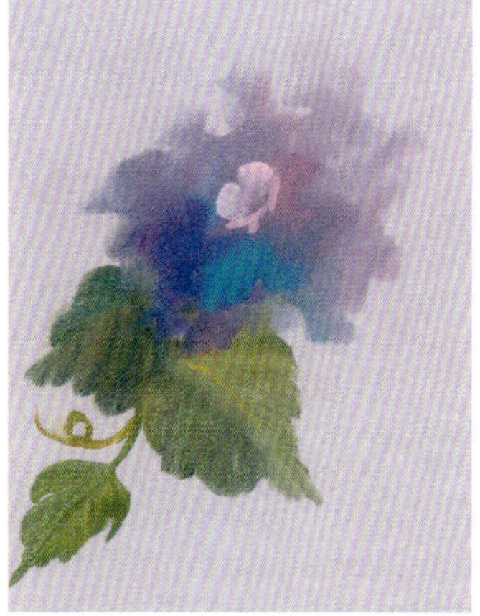

2. With a lighter color and the filbert brush, start in the lightest area of the flower and begin painting a few short-petaled florets.

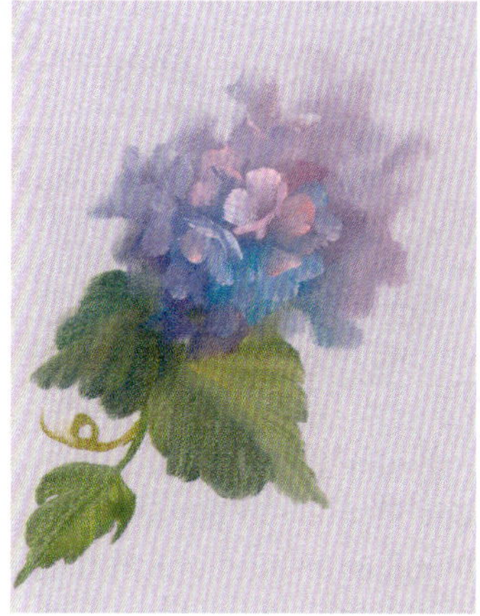

3. As you work away from the light area, paint just the indication of individual petals...

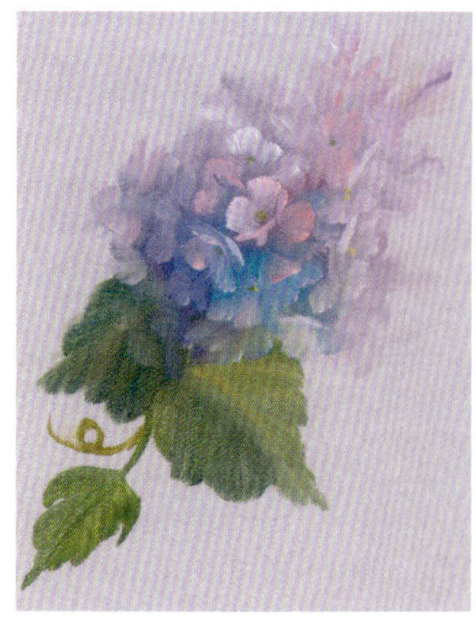

4. ...until the entire mass of florets is complete.

How to Paint a Cluster of Small Flowers

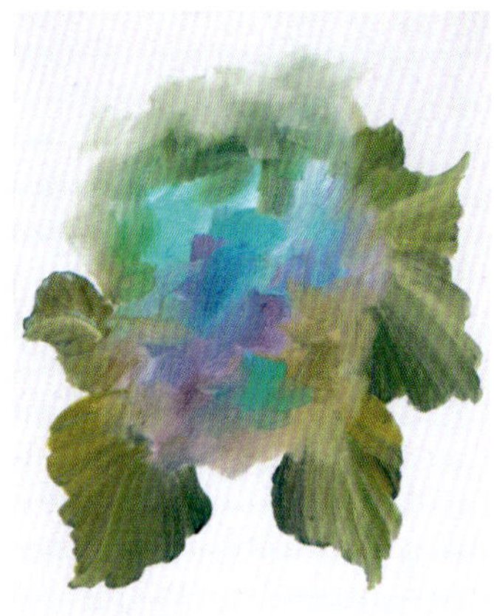

1. Use the 1/2" brush and criss-cross strokes to loosely underpaint the cluster of small flowers with a thin color of your choice.

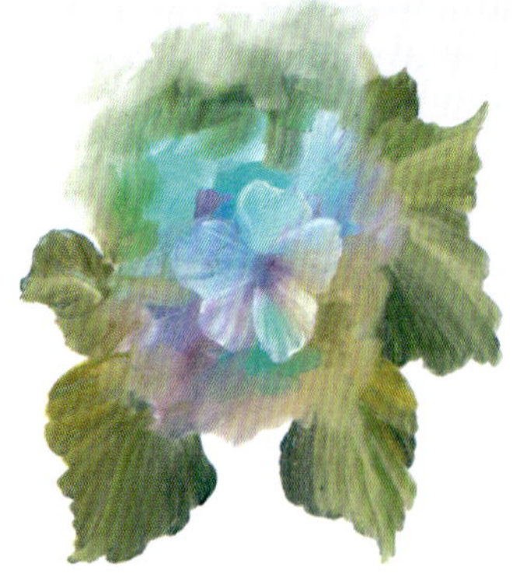

2. With a White and the filbert brush, start in the lightest area of the cluster and paint one small flower with overlapping strokes.

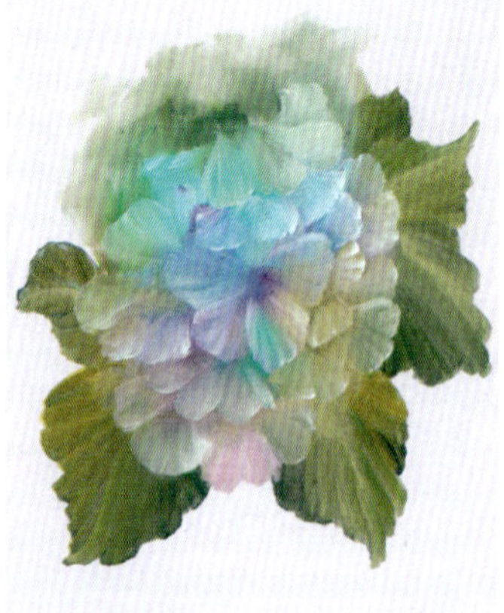

3. As you work away from the light area, paint just the indication of individual petals...

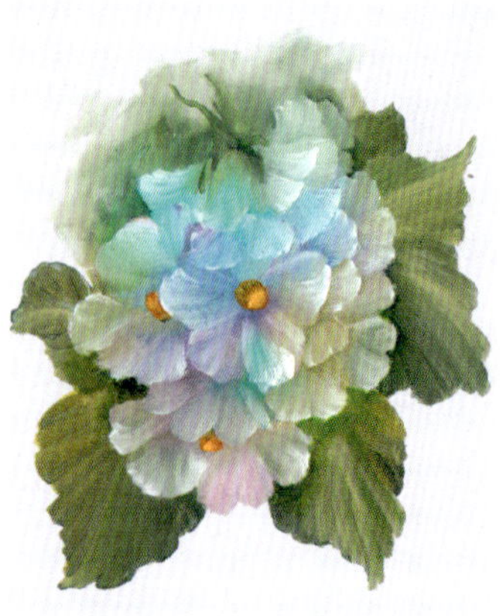

4. ...until the entire cluster of small flowers is complete. Add Orange centers with dots of Yellow highlights.

How to Paint a Basic Rose

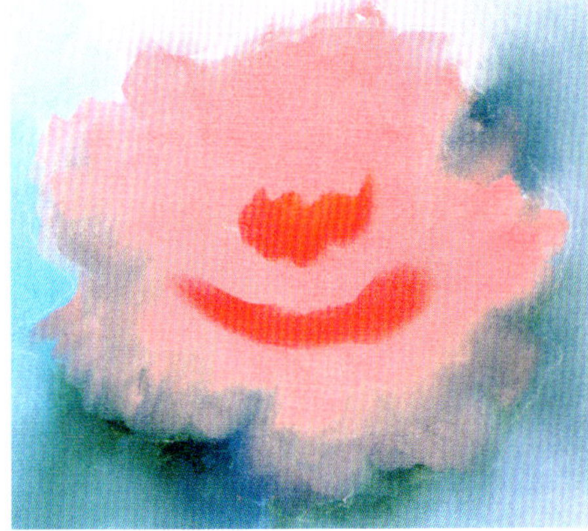

1.With the 3/4" brush, underpaint the flower with a thin mixture of Oil Paint Medium and Pink, Orange, Yellow or color of choice. Add Alizarin Crimson to the center...

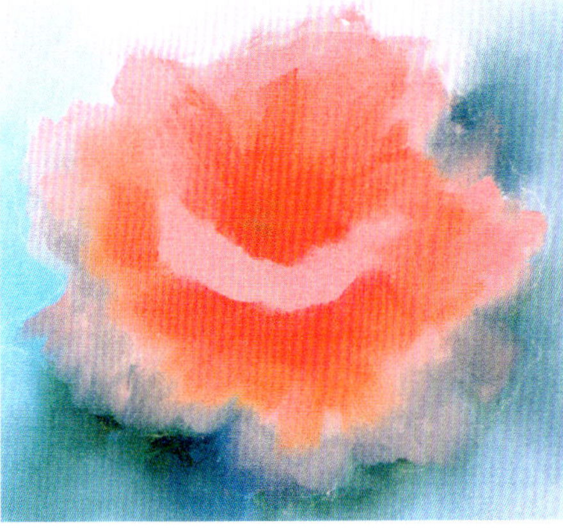

2. ...and under the cup of the rose. Then fan the dark color out from the center of the rose and from under the cup of the rose.

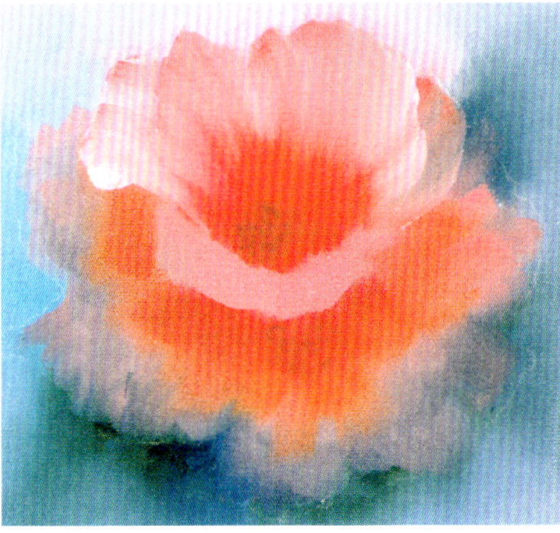

3. With White, start at the top of the rose, and create four large petals with overlapping strokes, all directed towards the center of the flower.

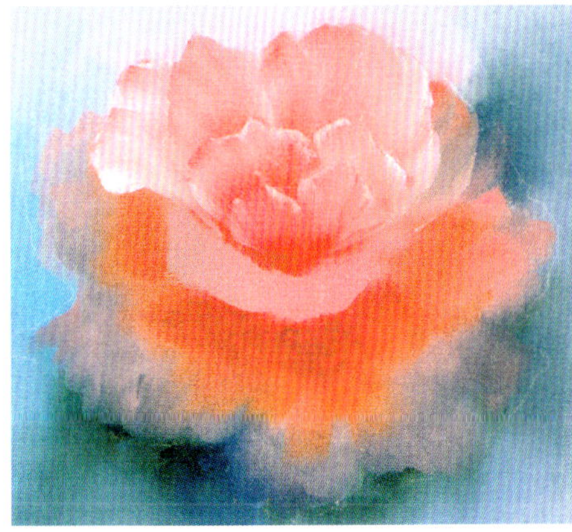

4. Thinking of each petal as fan shaped and working towards the center of the rose, add a second and third row of smaller petals.

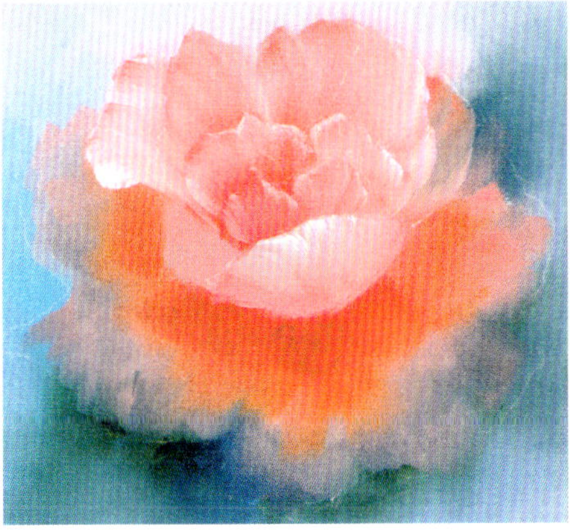

5. With White, "fold" up a lower front petal...

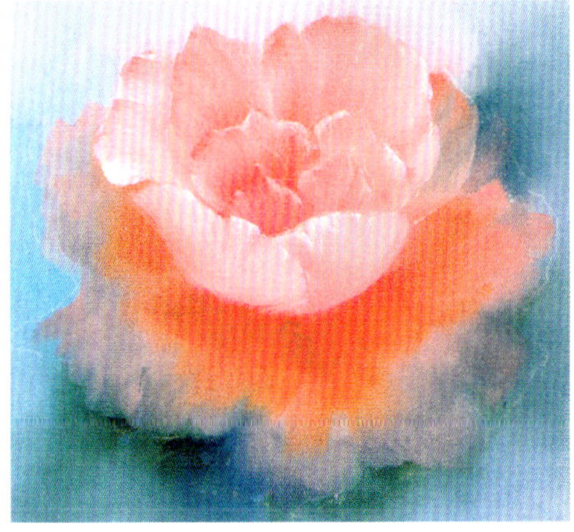

6. ...then add the second folded-up petal to form the cup of the rose.

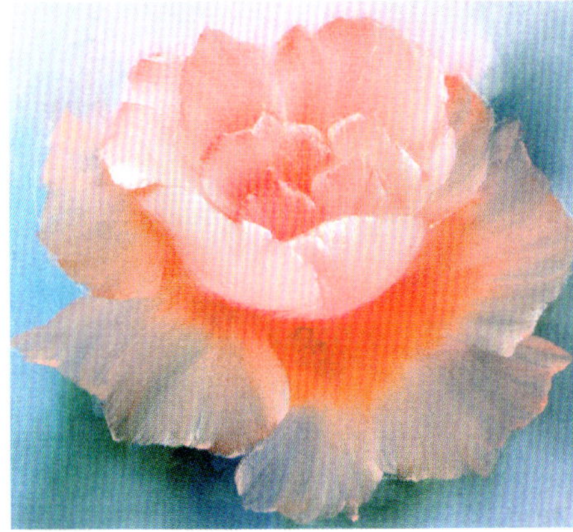

7. With White, add the lower petals, allowing the brush to pull in the foliage colors, creating the illusion of transparency.

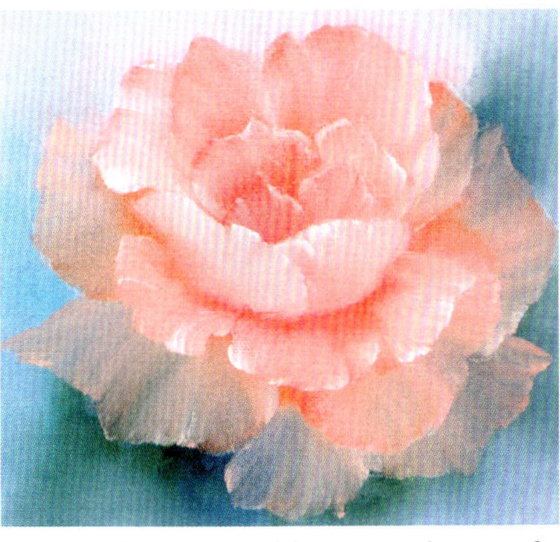

8. Use White to add a second row of petals at the base of the rose. Finally, add additional highlights, ruffles and folds, if desired,...

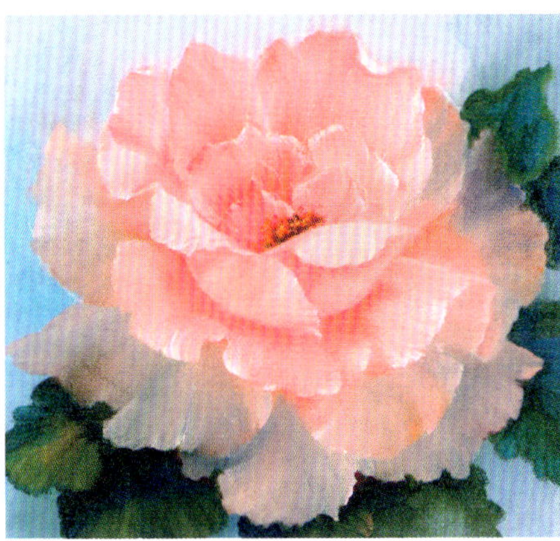

9. ...then use Alizarin Crimson to add the dark stamens in the center of the rose. Highlight the stamens with Yellow.

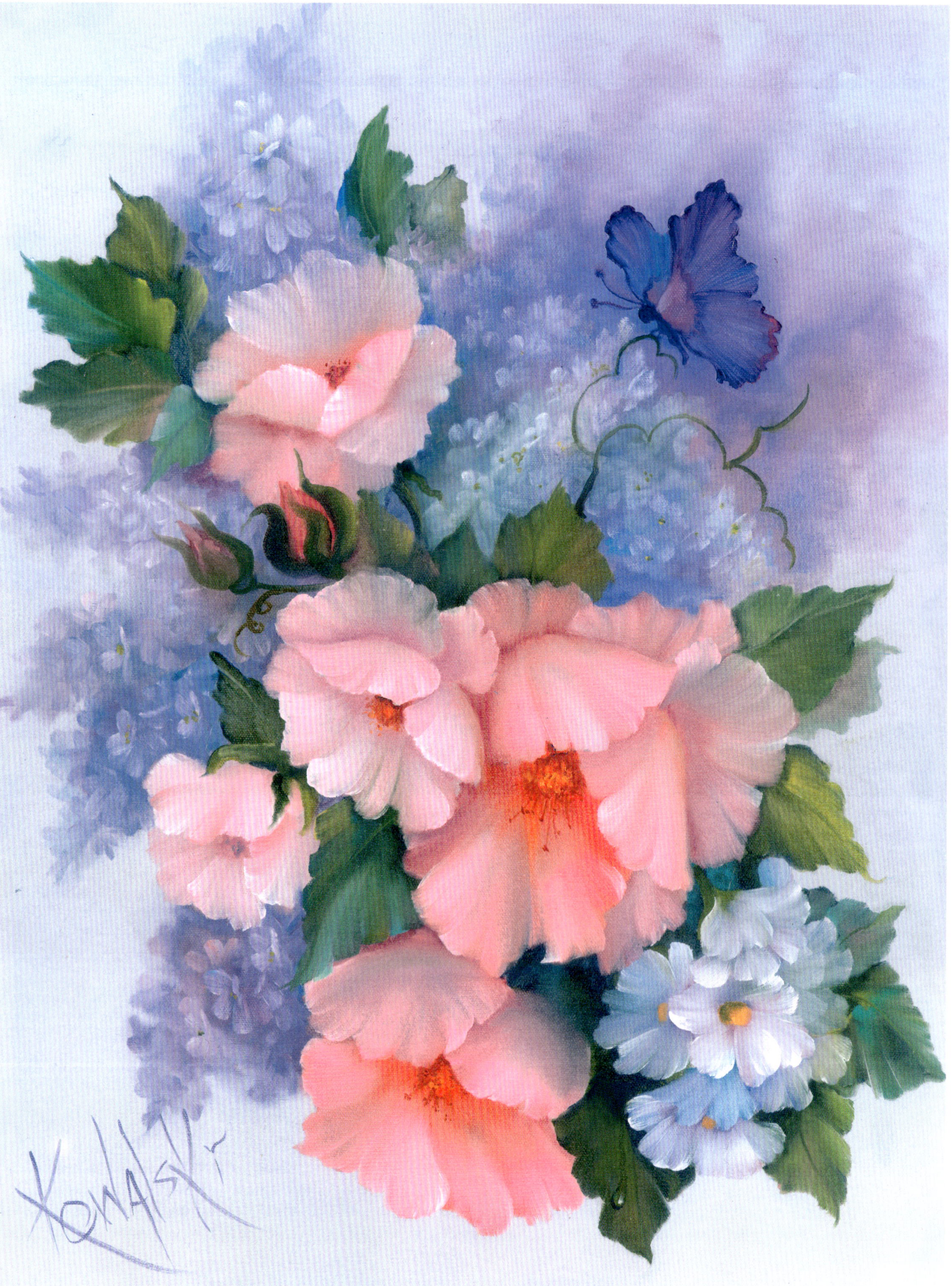
Kowalski

1. Riot of Posies

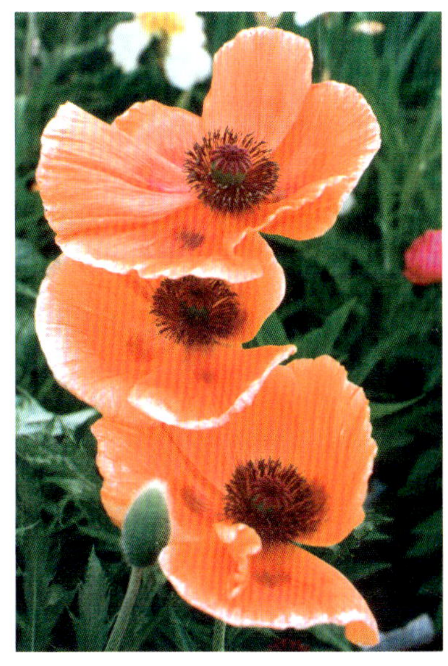

A wonderful first-time painting for those who are experiencing the Joy of Painting Flowers for the first time. For the more experienced painter, a chance to express your creativity with abandon. These posies are the Basic Flower and are pure fantasy flowers - no rules to break - and can be painted any color with as many petals as you like. Try Yellow, Purple or Red! The painting is designed to contain all of the basic components of a floral painting: basic flowers, small flowers, leaves, buds and a clusters of florets. Once you master these basic brushstrokes, you will be limited only by your imagination. The butterfly was added with little detail, allowing you the opportunity to experiment with color and design. Enjoy!

Materials:

Bob Ross Soft Oil Colors:
Alizarin Crimson
Cadmium Yellow Light
Cadmium Orange
Dusty Rose
Flower Pink
Mauve
Sap Green
Titanium White
Turquoise
Ultramarine Blue

Bob Ross Mediums:
Liquid Opal
Bob Ross Oil Paint Medium
Bob Ross Odorless Thinner

Bob Ross Brushes:
1" Landscape Brush
3/4" Floral Brush
1/2" Floral Brush
Floral Filbert Brush
Small Round Floral Brush
#2 Liner Brush

Other Materials:
Bob Ross Disposable Floral Palette
1 Canvas (18x24)

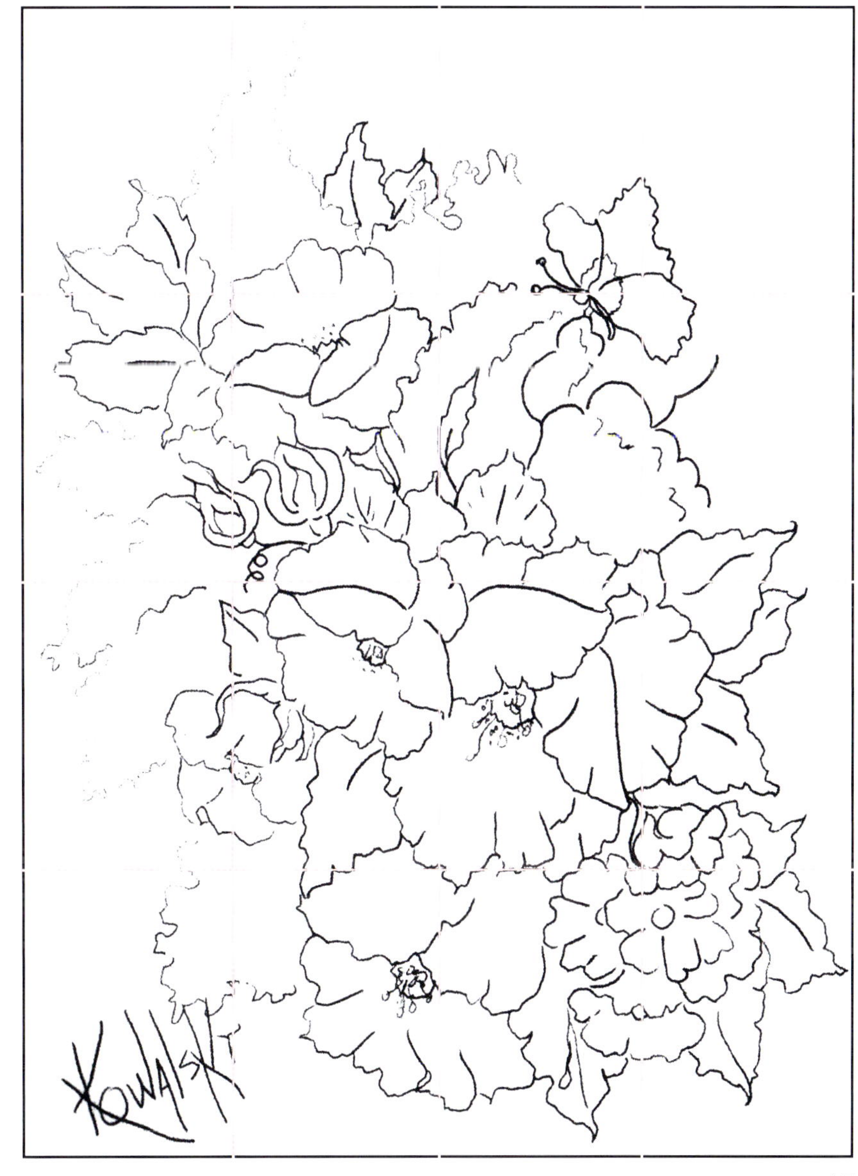

1. Riot of Posies

Progressional Steps

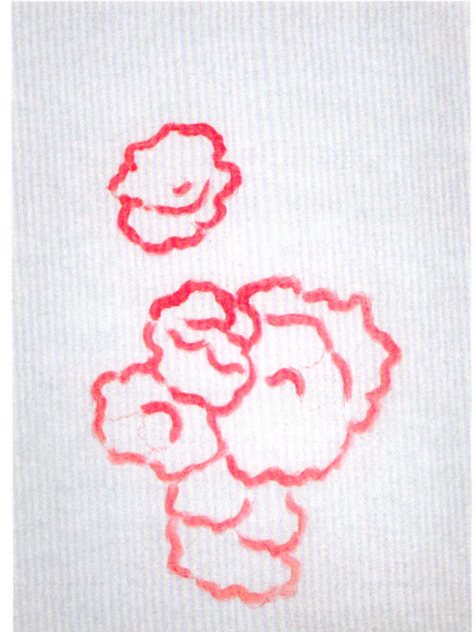

1. Lightly sketch the flower placement with thinned Pink on the small round brush. With the 1" brush, add Liquid Opal to the background.

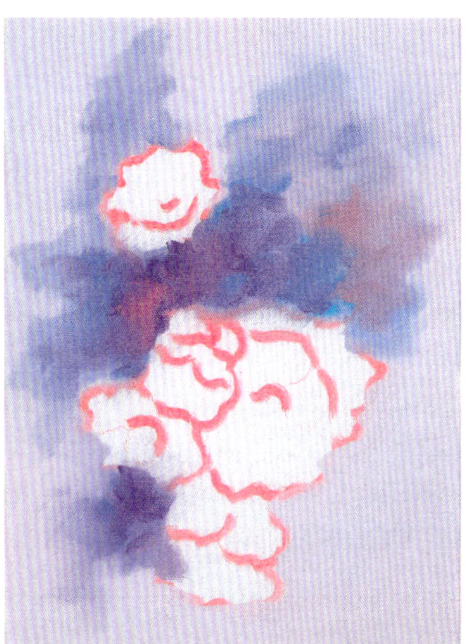

2. With the 1/2" brush and loose criss-cross strokes, underpaint the lilacs with various mixtures of Mauve, Turquoise, Blue and Dusty Rose. *Refer to Cluster Flowers in the Basic How-To Photo Instructions.*

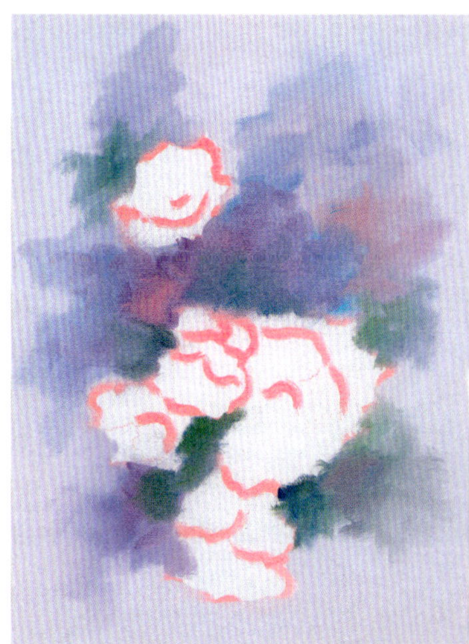

3. Add mixtures of Blue and Green to suggest foliage. Then, use the filbert brush and White to randomly suggest individual lilac blossoms.

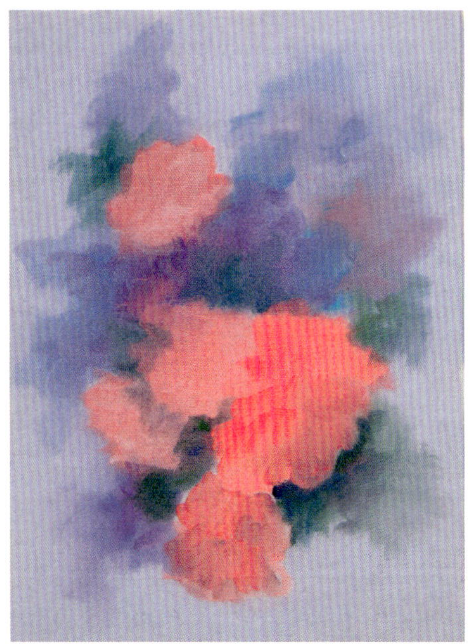

4. Referring to the *Basic Flower* in the *Basic How-To Photo Instructions,* underpaint the three flowers on the left side with thinned Dusty Rose. The flowers on the right are underpainted with Flower Pink.

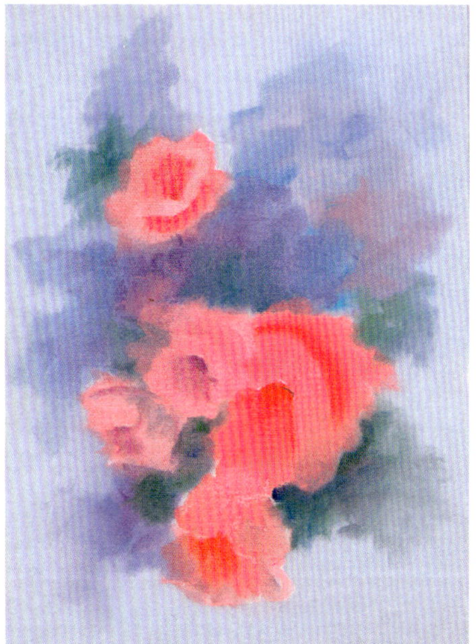

5. Add a mixture of Crimson and Mauve to the shadowed areas - Crimson and Orange to the two posies on the right side. Fan the color out from the center and blend with a clean dry 1/2" brush.

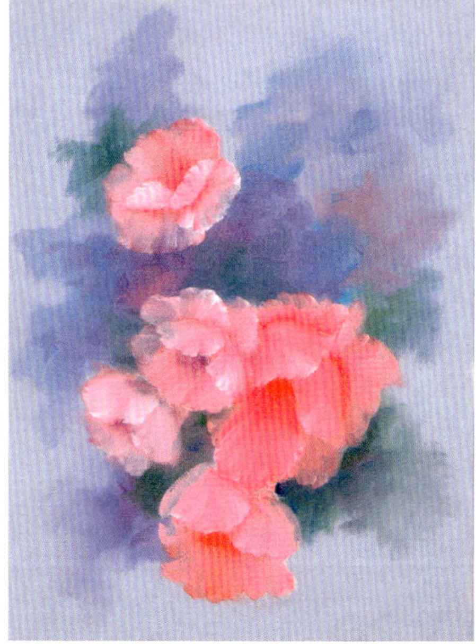

6. With the 1/2" brush, highlight the flowers, one petal at a time, with White. Starting at the out-side edge of each petal, direct a series of overlapping strokes towards the center of the flower.

1. Riot of Posies

Progressional Steps

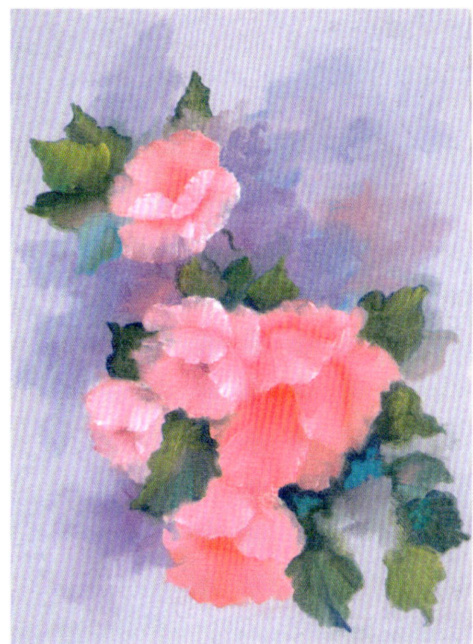

7. Referring to the *Basic Leaves in the Basic How-To Photo Instructions*, add leaves with mixtures of Green, Blue and Yellow. Then, underpaint the cluster of small flowers, adding Mauve, Turquoise and White to the leaf mixtures.

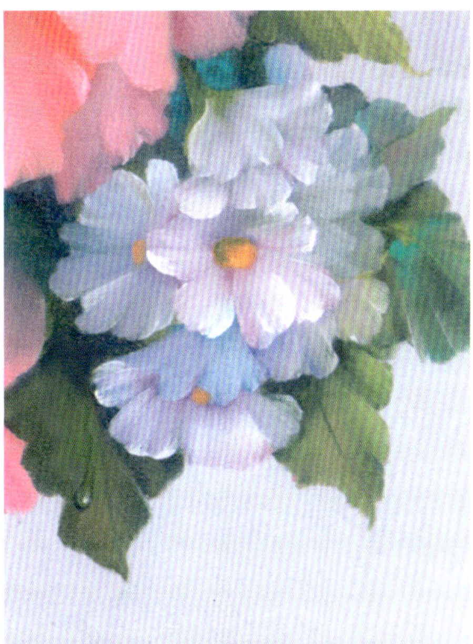

8. Highlight the small flowers with the filbert brush and White. The centers are a mixture of Yellow, Orange and Green. *Refer to the Cluster of Small Flowers in the Basic How-To Photo Instructions.*

9. Sketch the butterfly with the small round brush and a thin mixture of Mauve and Blue. Add Pink to the base of his wings and the outside edge of his lower wings.

10. With a clean, dry filbert brush and very little pressure, pull the paint in towards the body of the butterfly, creating the illusion of transparency.

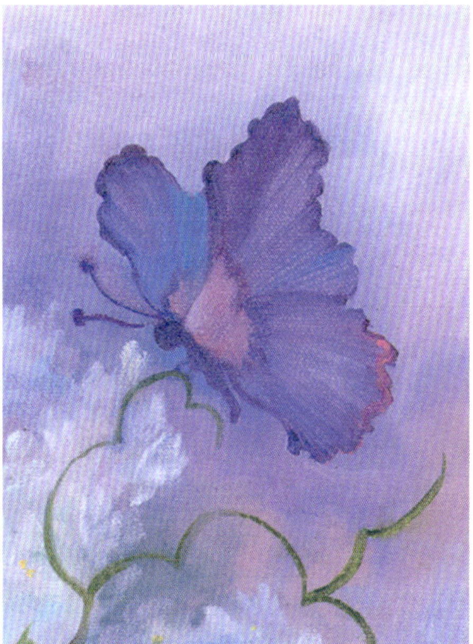

11. Again, use the small round brush and the dark mixture of Blue and Mauve to add the body, legs and antennas of the butterfly.

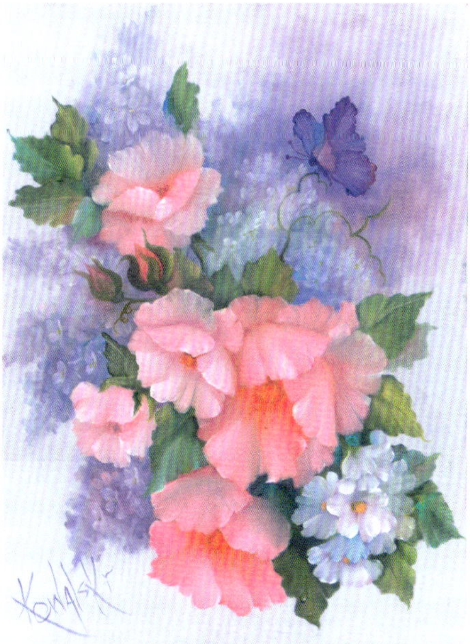

12. Add final details: buds, stems, twigs, tendrils, water drop; but most importantly, use the liner brush and thinned color to add your signature.

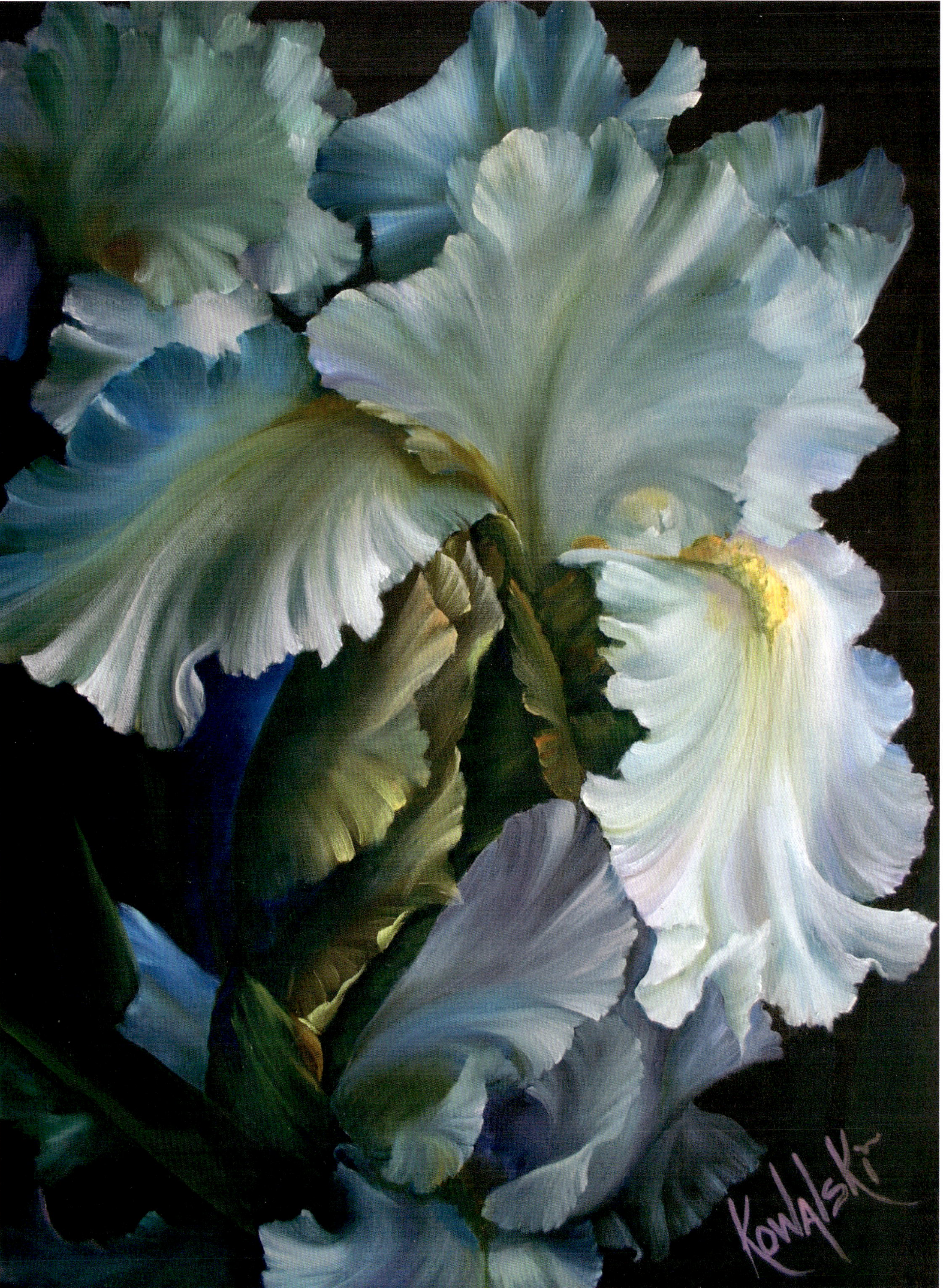
Kowalski

2. Midnight Iris

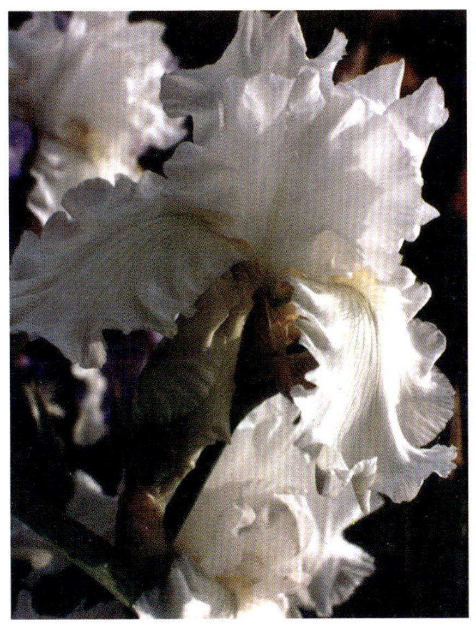

Using your own photographs as inspiration is one of the most satisfying aspects of floral painting and photography! A simple White iris becomes very dramatic when seen through the eyes of a camera.

Materials:

Bob Ross Soft Oil Colors:
Alizarin Crimson
Cadmium Yellow Light
Cadmium Orange
Cadmium Red Light
Mauve
Sap Green
Titanium White
Turquoise
Ultramarine Blue

Bob Ross Mediums:
Bob Ross Oil Paint Medium
Bob Ross Odorless Thinner
Black Gesso

Bob Ross Brushes:
1" Landscape Brush
3/4" Floral Brush
1/2" Floral Brush
Floral Filbert Brush
Small Round Floral Brush
#2 Liner Brush

Other Materials:
Bob Ross Disposable Floral Palette
1 Canvas (18x24)
Foam Applicator

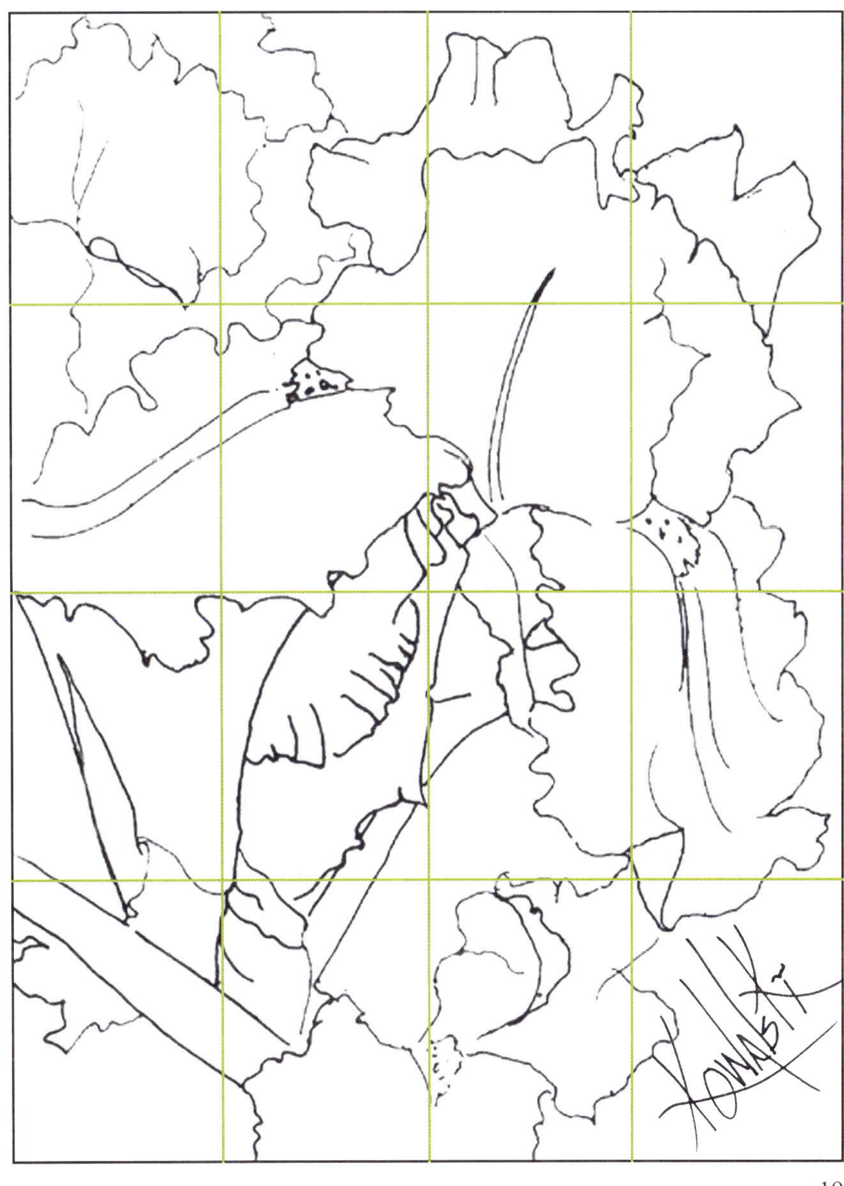

2. Midnight Iris

Progressional Steps

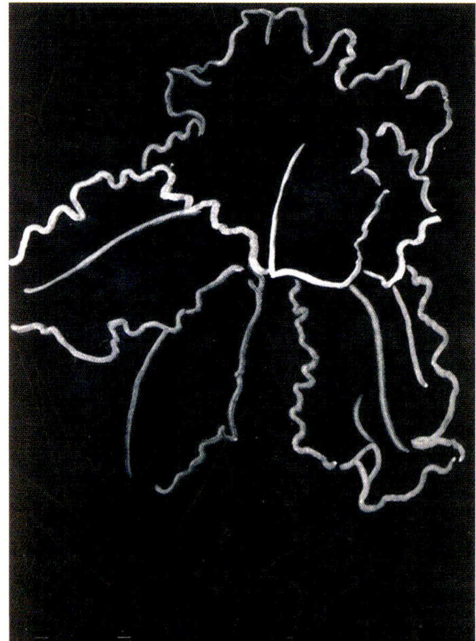

1. Begin by using the foam applicator to cover the entire canvas with a thin, even coat of Black Gesso and allow to dry completely. With a thin mixture of White and paint thinner, use the small round brush to loosely sketch the iris.

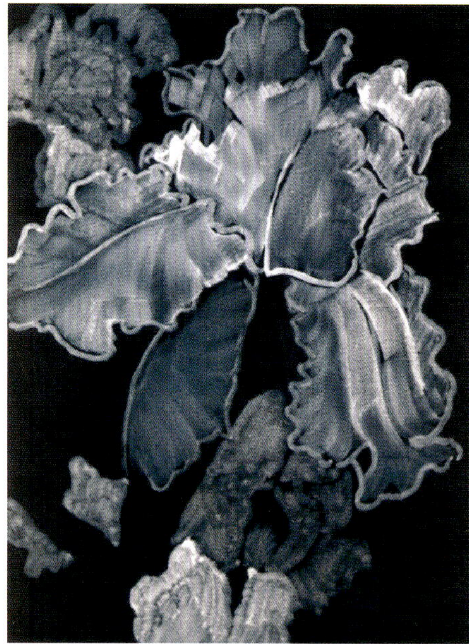

2. Use the 3/4" brush and a thin mixture of White and Odorless Paint Thinner to loosely underpaint the irises and bud. Then, carefully avoiding the flowers, use the 1" brush to apply a very, very small amount of Oil Paint Medium to the background.

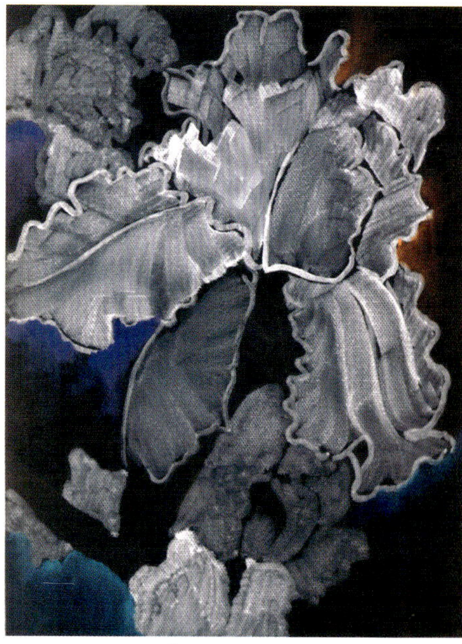

3. With the 1" brush, add small amounts of various mixtures of White, Turquoise, Mauve and Blue to the background.

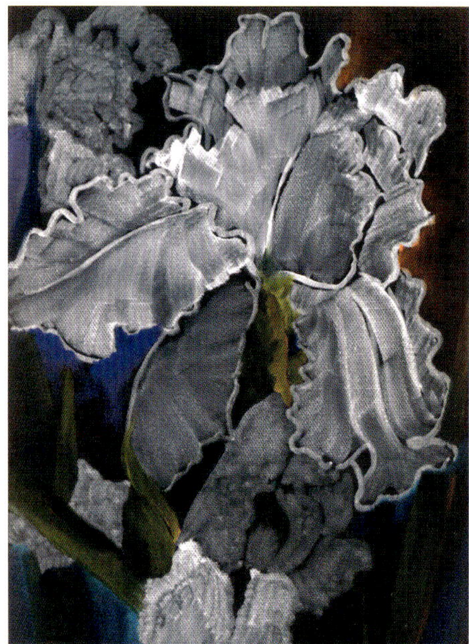

4. With the 1/2" and/or 3/4" brush, paint the leaves and stem with Blue and Green. Highlight with a very small amount of Yellow.

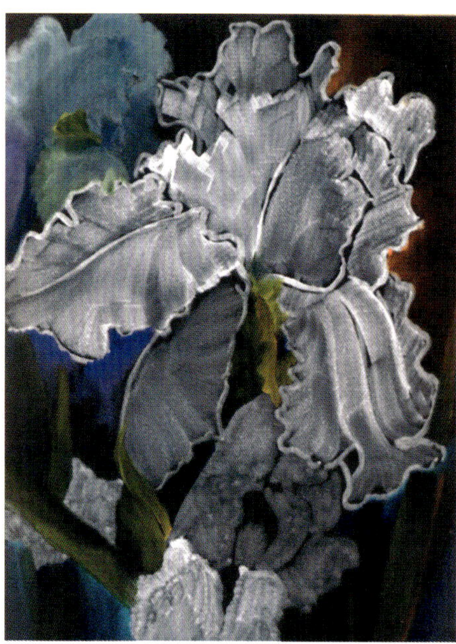

5. Continue using the 1/2" and 3/4" brushes to underpaint the background iris...

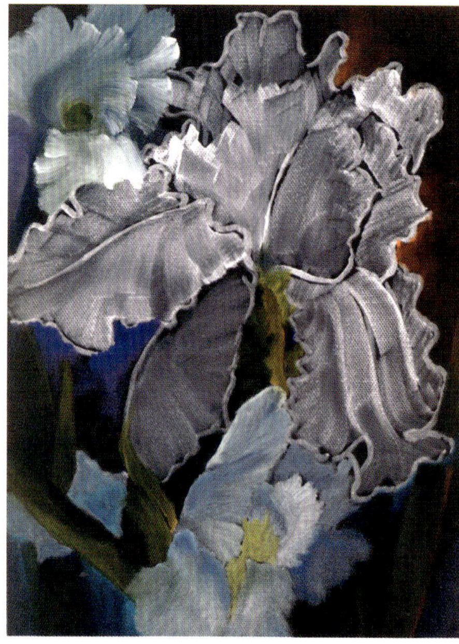

6. ...and the diffused foreground iris with various mixtures of White, Blue, Green and Turquoise. Add a small amount of Yellow to the centers of the irises.

Progressional Steps

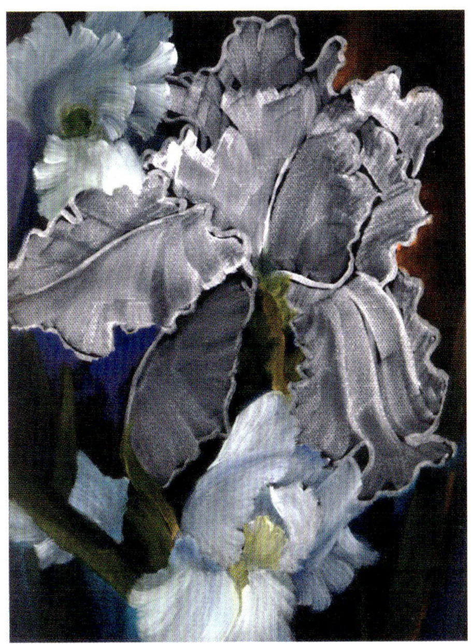

7. Use White to add subtle highlights to the background flowers.

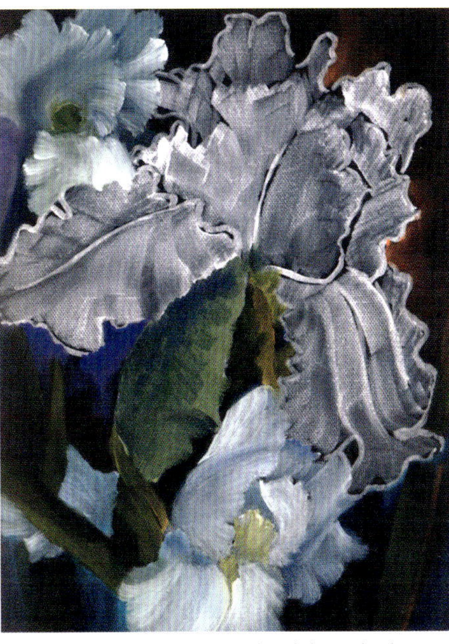

8. Underpaint the bud with a dark mixture of Green, Blue, Yellow and White.

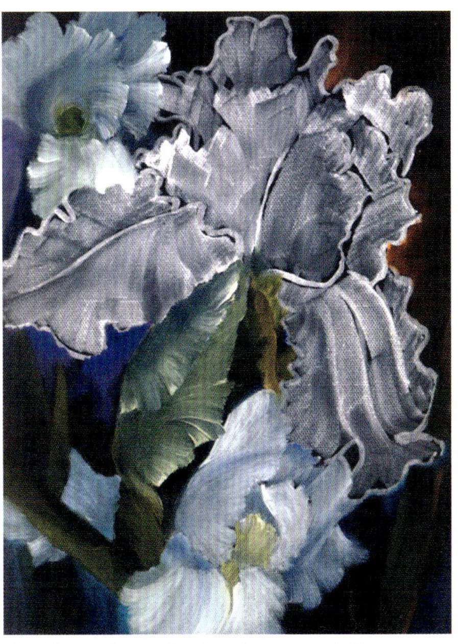

9. Complete the background flowers, the bud and foliage by adding final highlights with mixtures of White and Yellow.

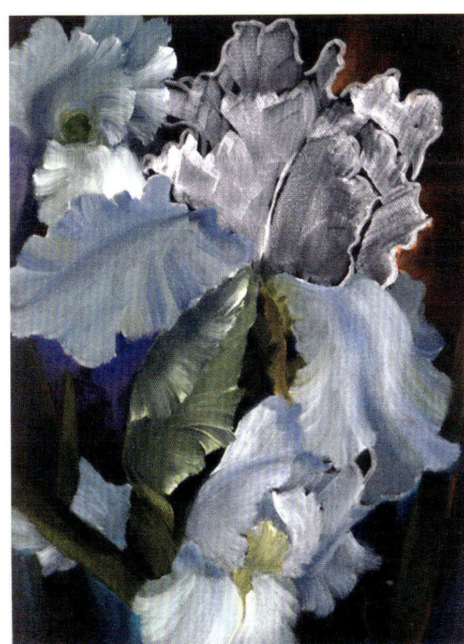

10. Paint the large, foreground iris, one petal at a time. Thinning the paint as necessary, use various mixtures of White, Blue, Green and Turquoise and the 1/2" and 3/4" brushes.

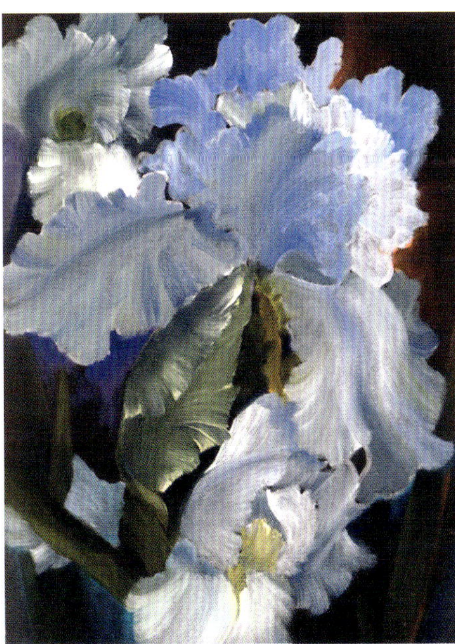

11. Starting at the outside edge of each petal, use long flowing strokes, all directed towards the center of the flower.

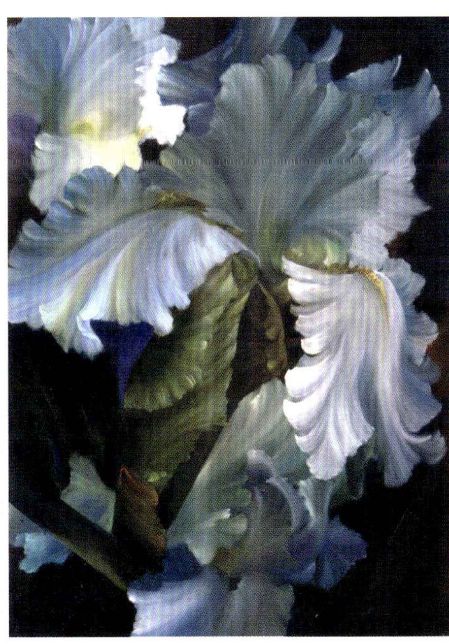

12. Final highlights are White and Yellow - shadowed areas are White, Blue and Green. Underpaint the 'beards' with a mixture of Green and Yellow. Highlight the furry beards with a mixture of White and Yellow.

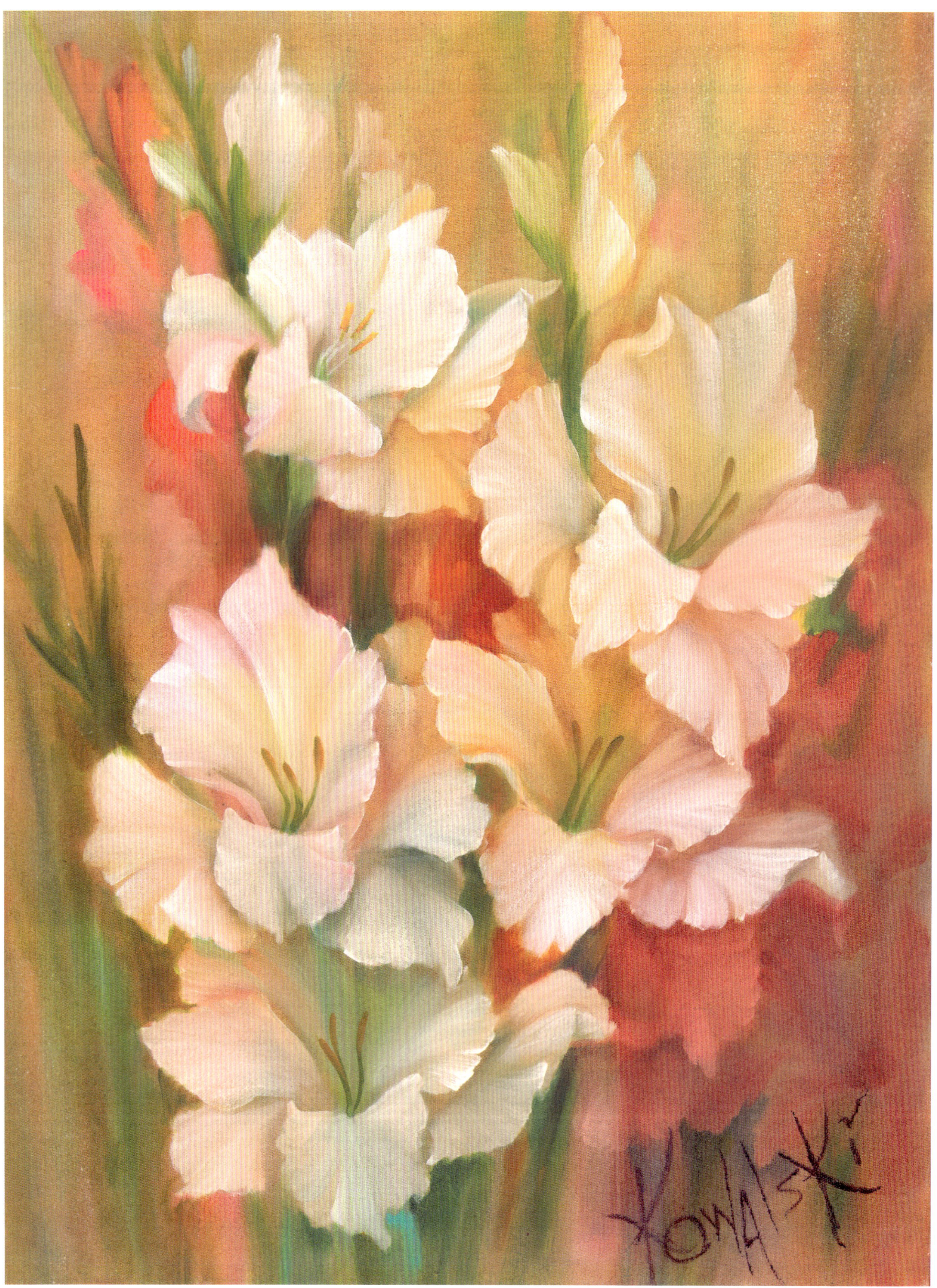
Kowalski

3. White Gladiolus

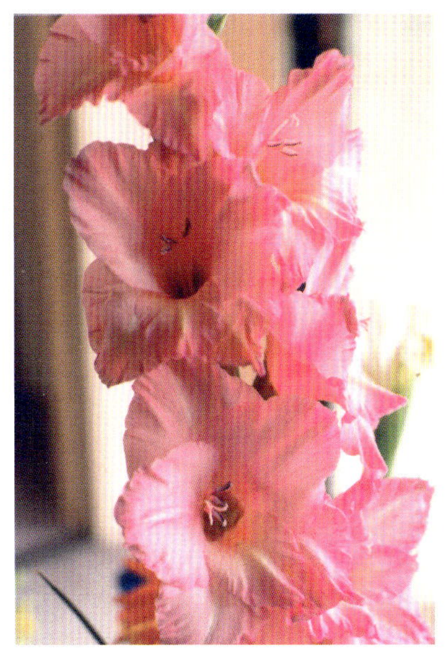

A good painting for a canvas gone bad. A happy accident. This painting started as less-than-pleasing multi-colored gladiolus. With the large two-inch brush and several swift brushstrokes, the flowers almost disappeared into the background. Then, transparent white gladiolus were painted over that diffused previous painting. The Joy of Painting Flowers - The Joy of Painting Flowers in oils!

Materials:

Bob Ross Soft Oil Colors:
Alizarin Crimson
Cadmium Yellow Light
Cadmium Orange
Dusty Rose
Mauve
Sap Green
Titanium White
Turquoise
Ultramarine Blue

Bob Ross Mediums:
Bob Ross Oil Paint Medium
Bob Ross Odorless Thinner

Bob Ross Brushes:
1" Landscape Brush
3/4" Floral Brush
1/2" Floral Brush
Floral Filbert Brush
Small Round Floral Brush
#2 Liner Brush

Other Materials:
Bob Ross Disposable Floral Palette
1 Canvas (18x24)

Painting Tip

Transfer the gladiolus pattern to waxed paper. Place the waxed pattern over your completed background and use a blunt pencil point to lightly 'impress' the pattern onto the wet canvas. This method will provide you with a clearly visible pattern that can easily be covered with the White outline paint.

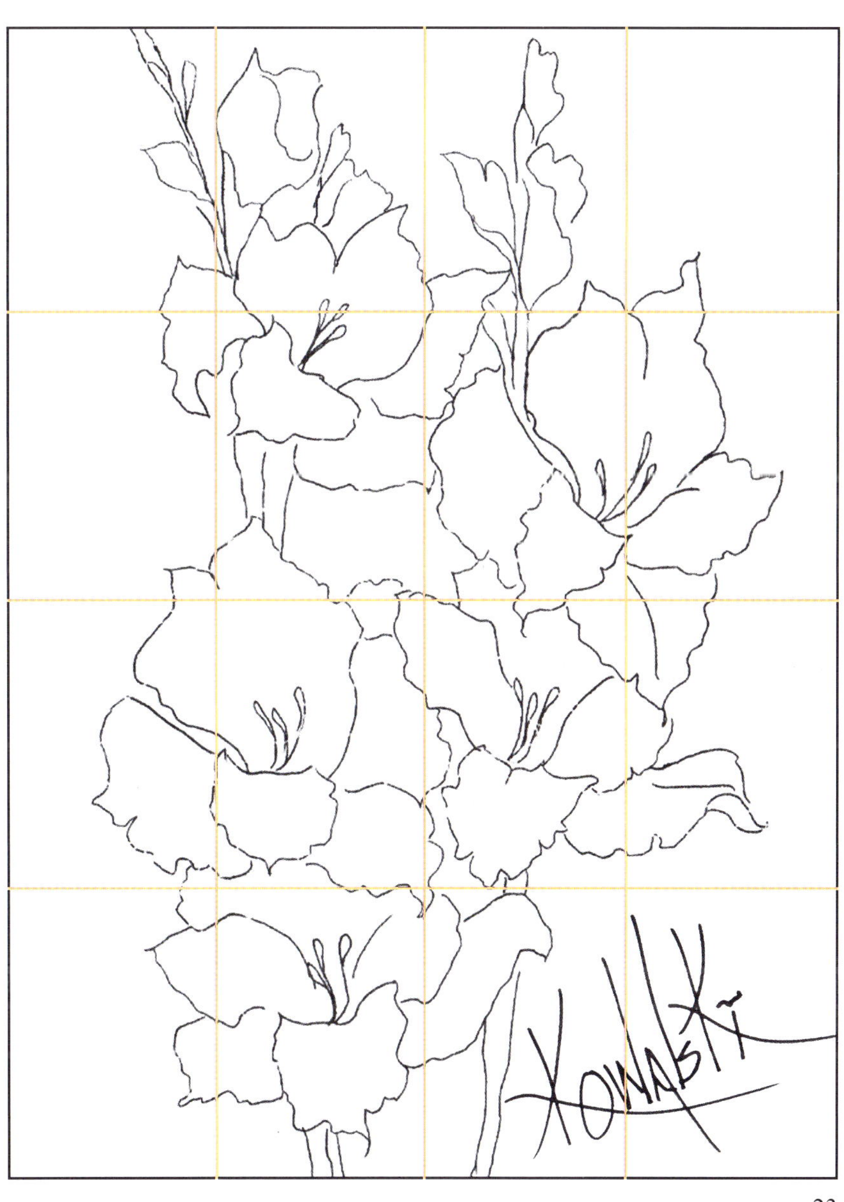

3. White Gladiolus

Progressional Steps

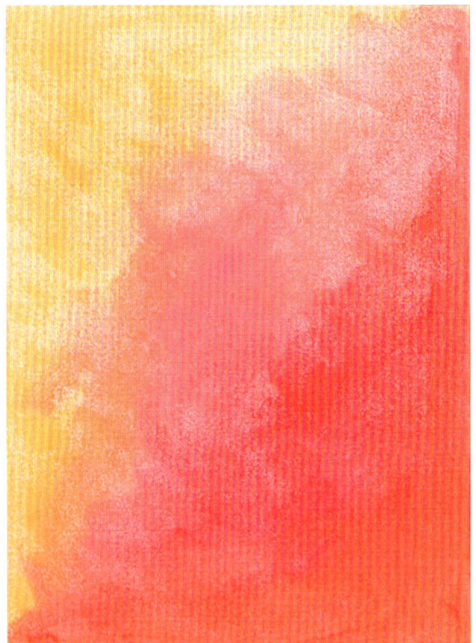

1. Use the 1" brush to coat the canvas with a very, very small amount of Oil Paint Medium. Then use loose criss-cross strokes to add Yellow, Flower Pink, Cadmium Red Light and Alizarin Crimson to the background.

2. Lightly blend with a clean, dry brush and criss-cross strokes.

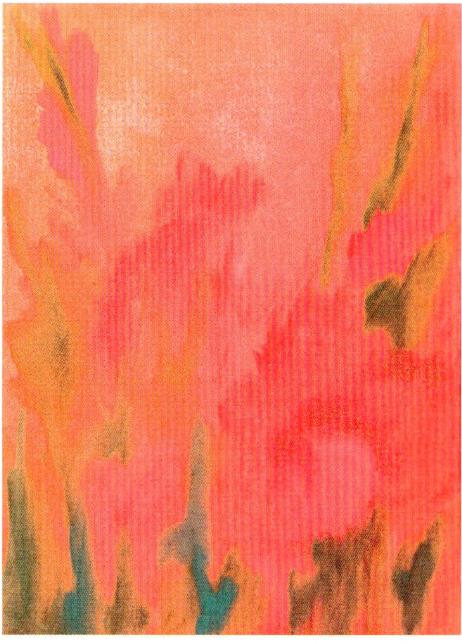

3. With the 3/4" brush, add just the suggestion of out-of-focus flowers to the background with loose glad-like strokes. Use Flower Pink, Cad Red Light, Crimson, Mauve, Green and Blue.

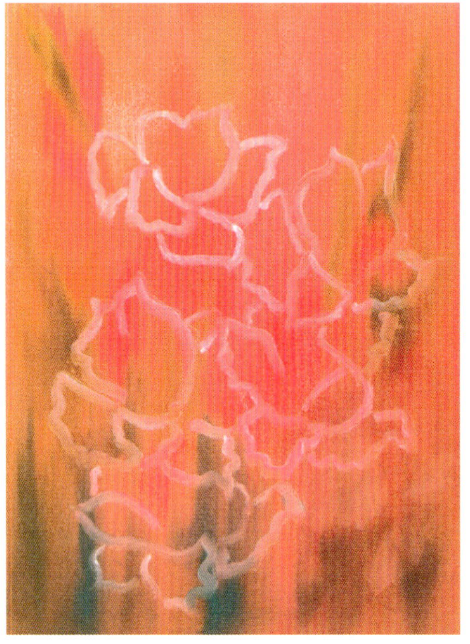

4. With a mixture of Oil Paint Medium and Titanium White, use the small round brush to loosely sketch the placement of each of the five blossoms.

Gladiola Closeup

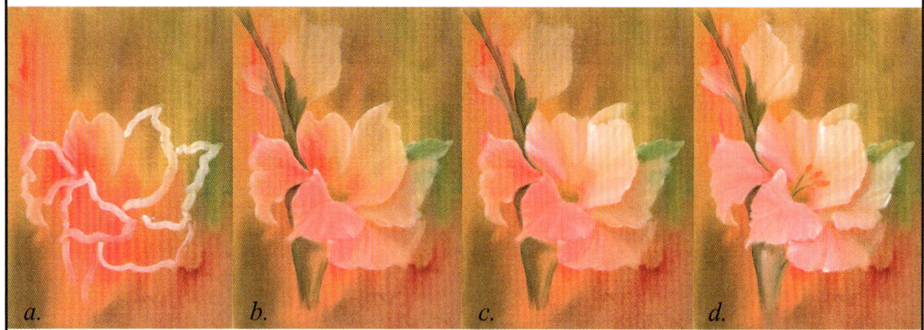

a. Sketch each flower with thinned White.

b. To underpaint each petal, use a clean, dry 1/2" brush to pull the outline paint in towards the center of the flower.

c. Complete each flower one petal at a time. Do not completely cover the background colors; this is the underpainting and should not be too light. Add the foliage and buds.

d. Add a very small amount of a mixture of Flower Pink and Sap Green to create the center of the flower. With Titanium White and the 1/2" brush, add final highlights. The stamens are Blue/Green, tipped with Yellow.

3. White Gladiolus

Progressional Steps

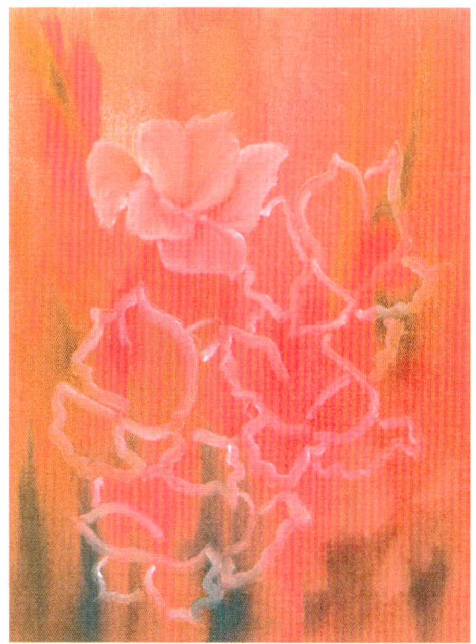

5. To underpaint each flower, use a clean, dry 1/2" brush to pull the outline paint in towards the center of the flower.

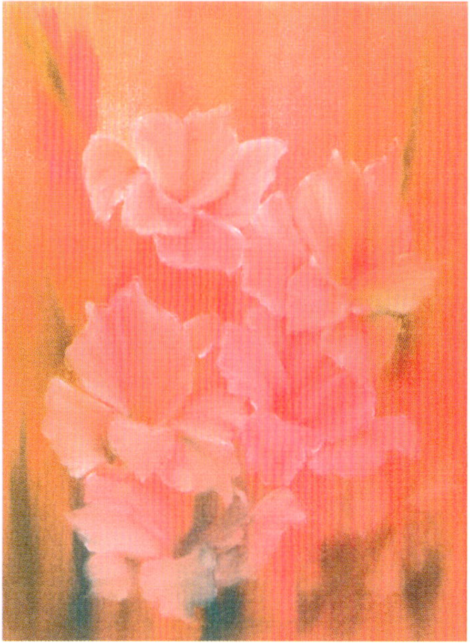

6. Working one petal at a time, use a series of long, overlapping strokes, pulling the White edges in towards the center of each flower.

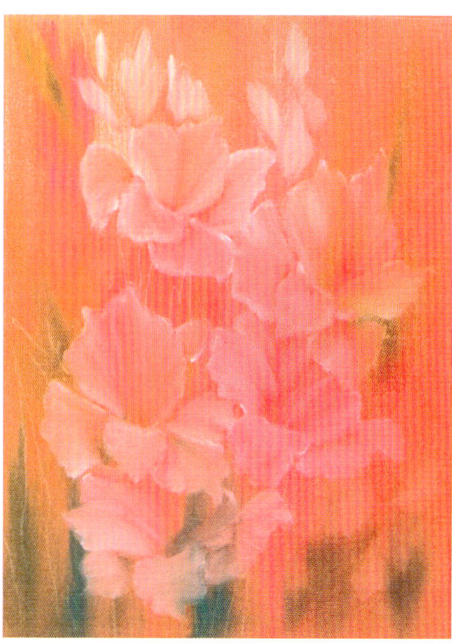

7. By not completely covering the background colors, with just a few brush strokes, you can create individual, transparent flowers and buds.

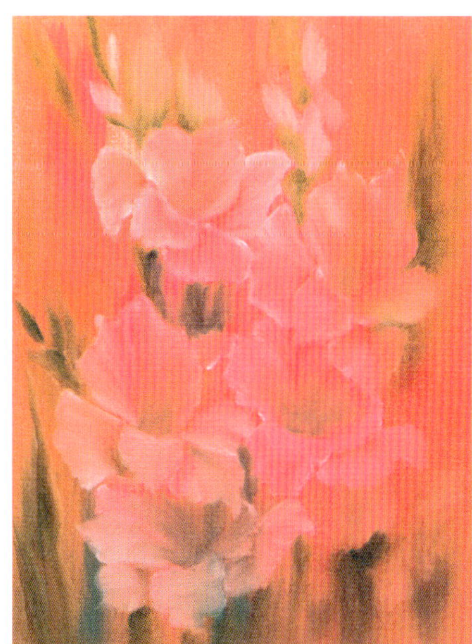

8. Add the stems and calyx with mixtures of Blue, Green and Yellow. Darken the centers of the flowers with Flower Pink and Green.

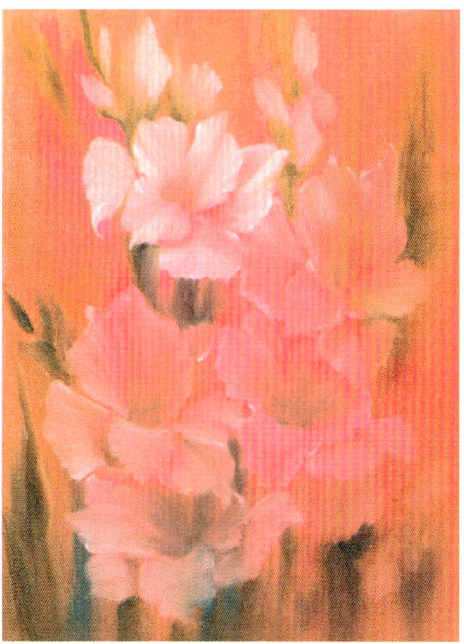

9. Use the 1/2" brush and/or the 3/4" brush to add highlights to each of the flowers with Titanium White.

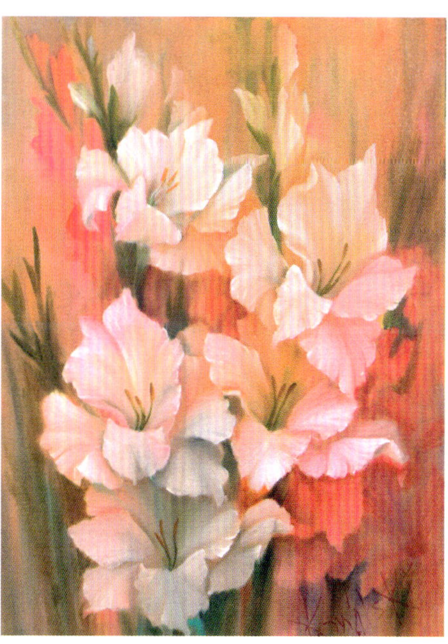

10. Finally, with the tip of the filbert brush, add Green stamens, tipped with Indian Yellow. Most importantly, sign your flowers with thinned color and the liner brush.

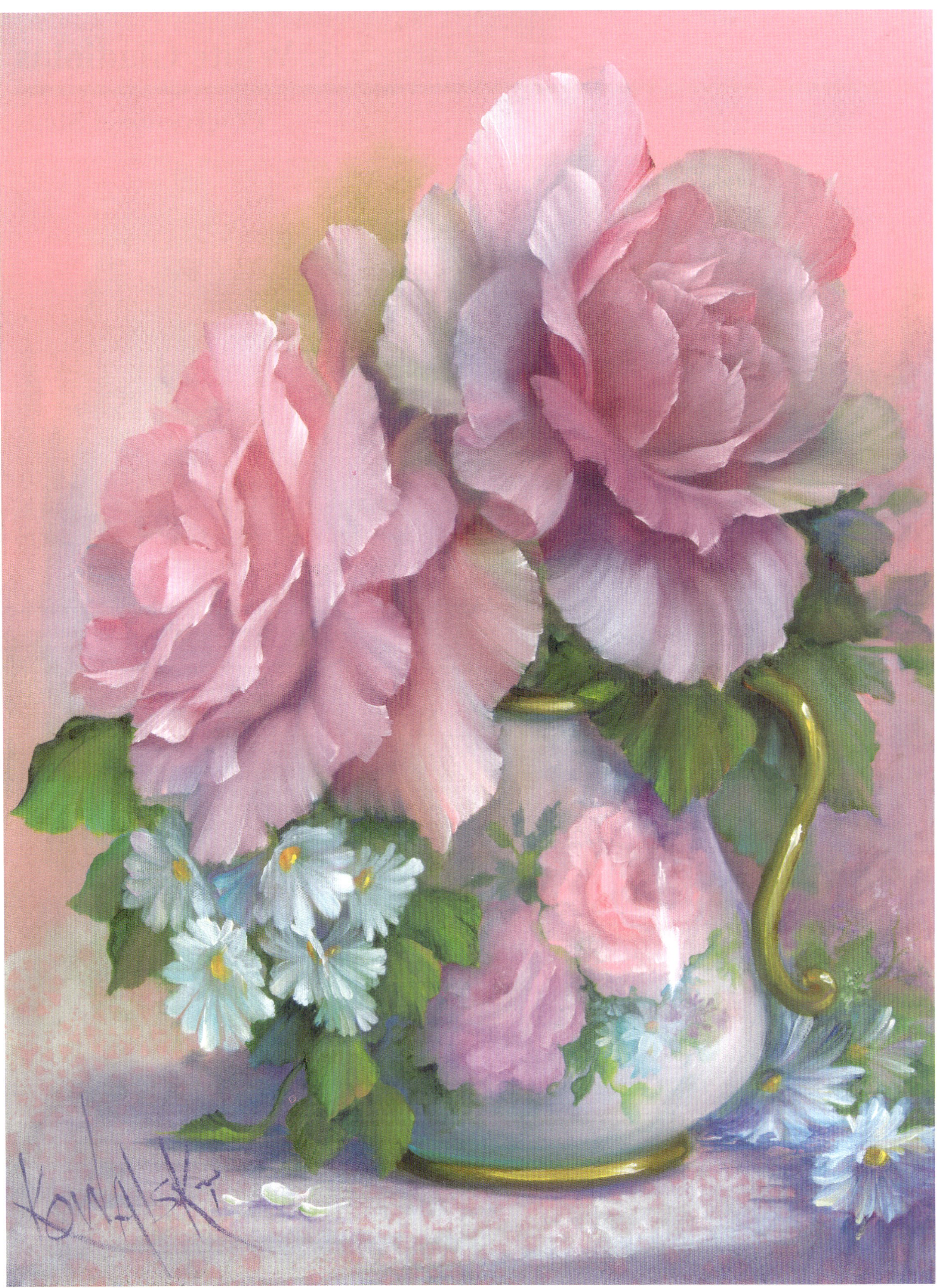
KOWALSKI

4. Roses in Roses

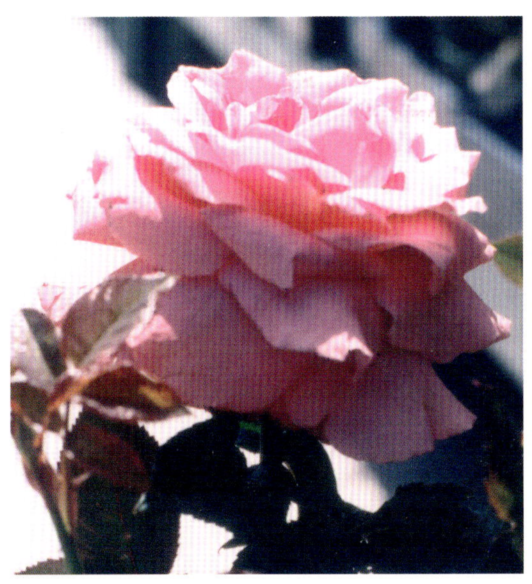

With a can of acrylic spray paint, you can create a painting that requires very little background work and, with just a few brush strokes, you can create the glittering gold accents on the ceramic pitcher. Roses come in many colors. Try yellow roses on a blue background with a lace tabletop and a ceramic pot decorated with yellow and orange roses.

Materials:

Bob Ross Soft Oil Colors:
Alizarin Crimson
Cadmium Yellow Light
Cadmium Orange
Dusty Rose
Mauve
Sap Green
Titanium White
Turquoise
Ultramarine Blue

Bob Ross Mediums:
Bob Ross Oil Paint Medium
Bob Ross Odorless Thinner

Bob Ross Brushes:
1" Landscape Brush
3/4" Floral Brush
1/2" Floral Brush
Floral Filbert Brush
Small Round Floral Brush
#2 Liner Brush

Other Materials:
Bob Ross Disposable Floral Palette
1 Canvas (18x24)
Acrylic Spray Paint, Pink
Paper Lace Doily
Masking Tape

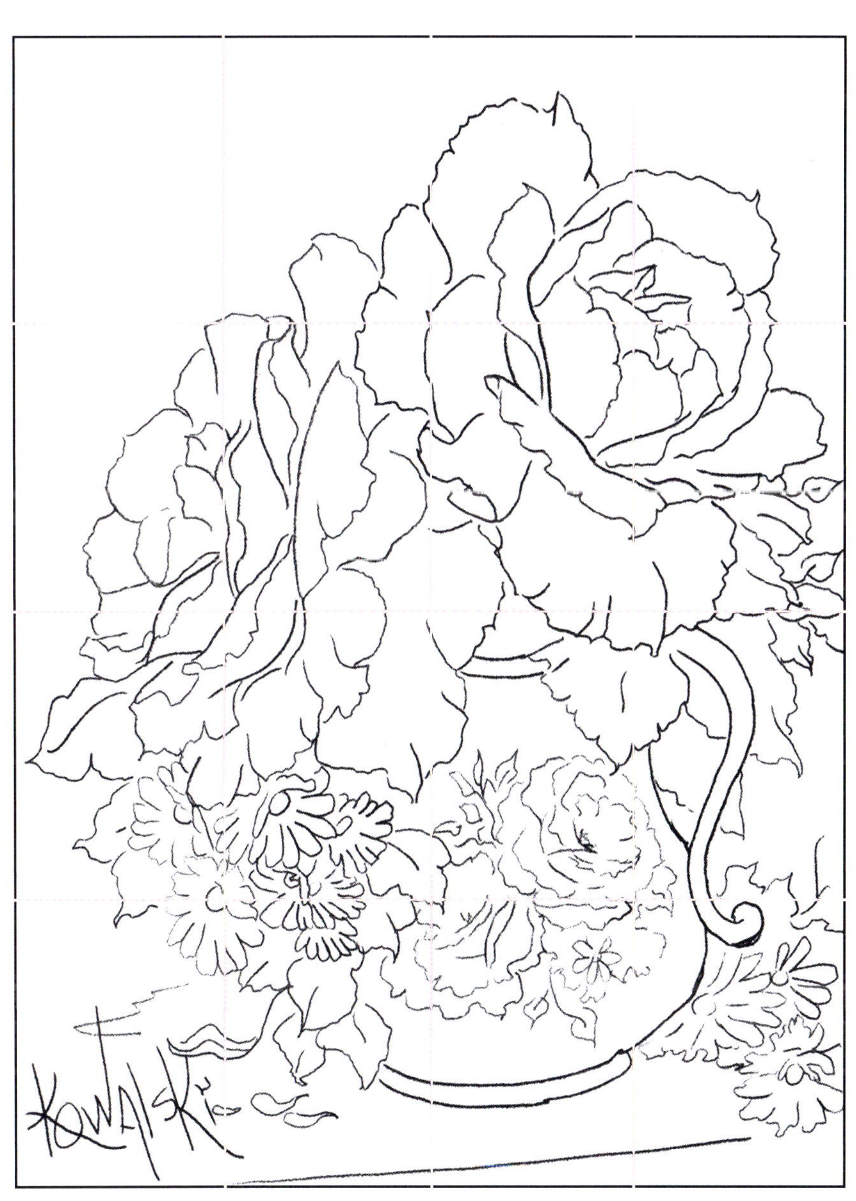

4. Roses in Roses

Progressional Steps

1. Prepare the canvas by using masking tape to adhere the paper doily to the lower portion of the canvas. Lightly spray the entire canvas with the Pink acrylic spray paint. Allow to dry completely. Remove the doily and voila! you have created a lace-covered tabletop.

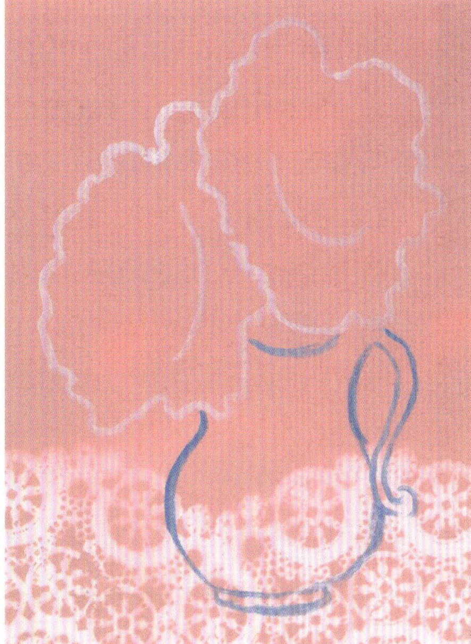

2. Apply a very, very small amount of Oil Paint Medium to the entire canvas, then use a thin mixture of Blue and Oil Paint Medium on the small round brush to lightly sketch the placement of the pitcher. Use thinned White to sketch the two large roses.

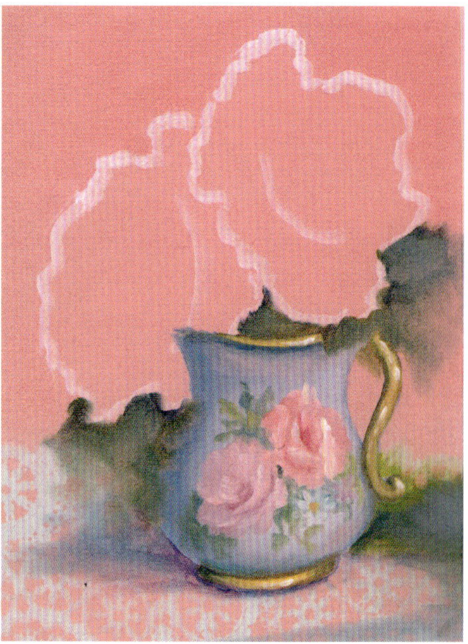

3. After painting the pitcher, use the 3/4" brush and mixtures of Blue and Green to loosely block in the foliage.

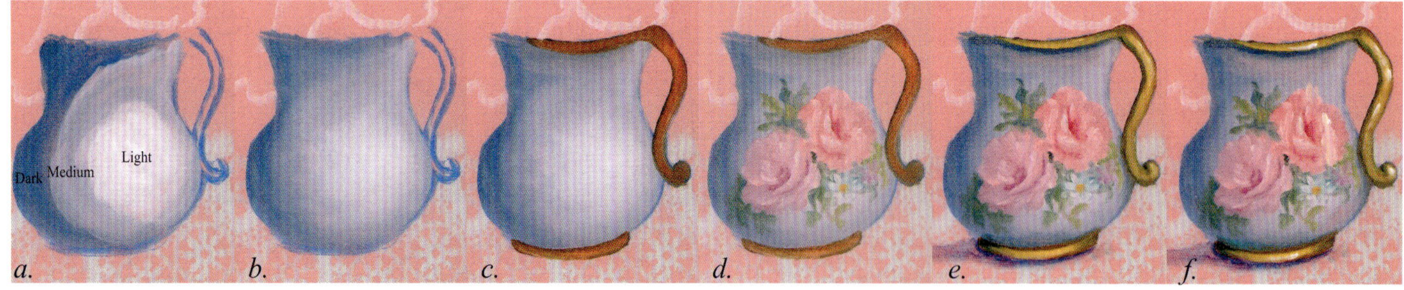

4. Painting the Gold-Trimmed Ceramic Pitcher

a. With the 3/4" brush and loose criss-cross strokes, paint the dark area of the pot with a mixture of Blue, Green, Turquoise and Mauve to which you have added a small amount of White. Add White to the mixture for the middle value of the pot. Then add more White which has been tinted with Dusty Rose for the light value.

b. With a clean, dry brush, use criss-cross strokes to merge the three values. Use the fan brush with sweeping, horizontal strokes to soften the entire pot.

c. Underpaint the gold trim with the filbert brush and a mixture of Orange and Green.

d. Use the 1/2" brush and the filbert brush to paint roses and small flowers on the pot with various mixtures of Pink, Mauve, Green, Yellow and White. Blend lightly with a clean, dry fan brush.

e. Add the light area of the gold trim with a mixture Yellow and White.

f. Use pure White to add highlight sparkles to the pot and the gold trim.

4. Roses in Roses

Progressional Steps

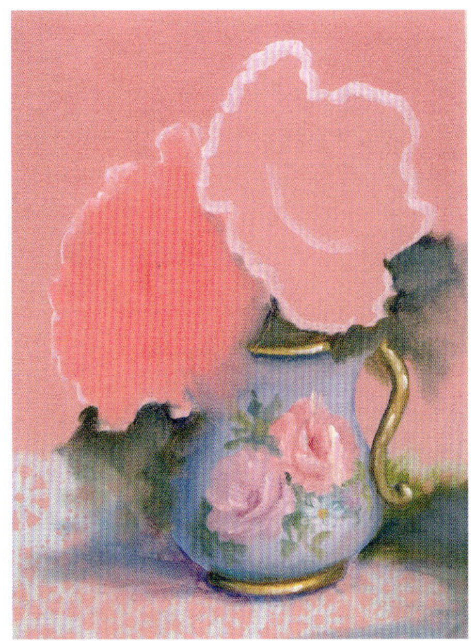

5. Loosely underpaint the first rose with the 3/4" brush and Dusty Rose which has been thinned with a small amount of Oil Paint Medium. *Refer to the Basic Rose in the Basic How-To Photographs.*

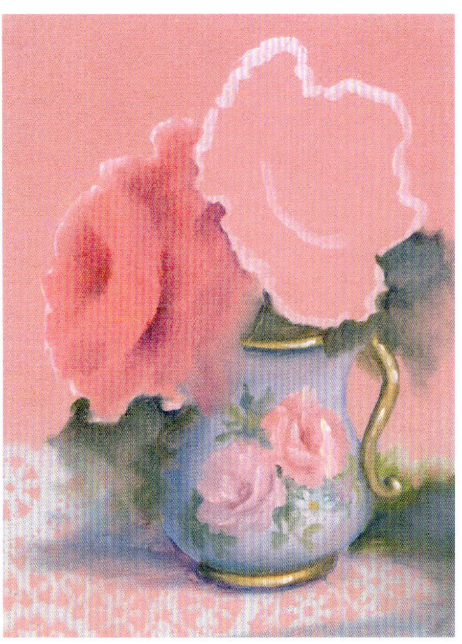

6. Add the shadowed areas of the rose with Alizarin Crimson.

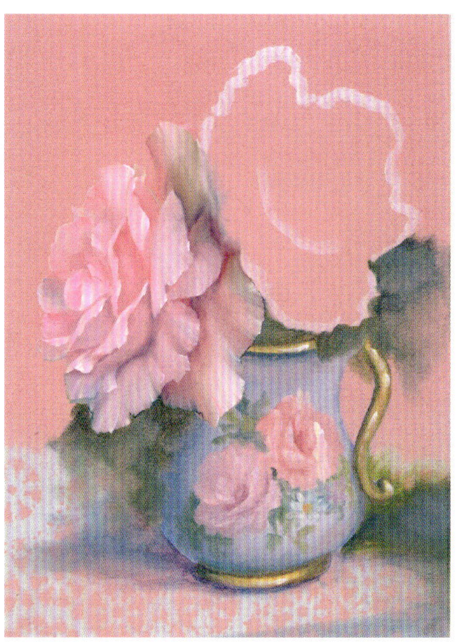

7. Use mixtures of White and Dusty Rose to create individual petals, then add final highlights with White.

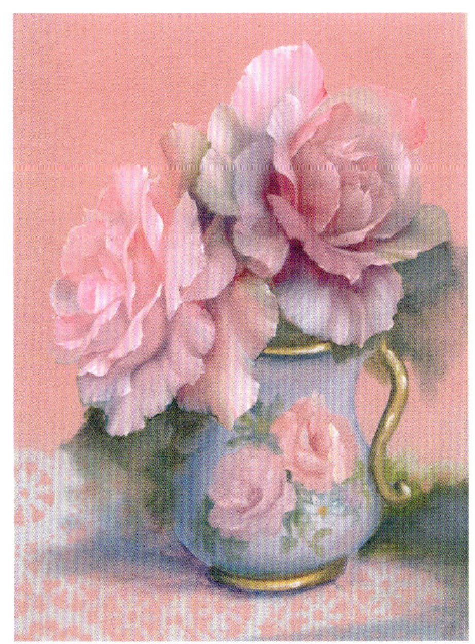

8. Add the second rose with thinned Dusty Rose; a mixture of Alizarin Crimson and Mauve for the shadowed areas. Be sure to allow your brush to 'pull' in the foliage colors, creating the illusion of transparency.

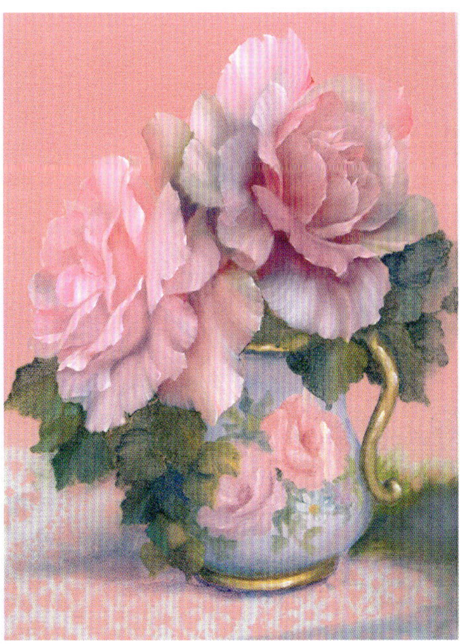

9. After completing the second rose, add clusters of leaves with mixtures of Blue, Green, Yellow, Alizarin Crimson and Turquoise.

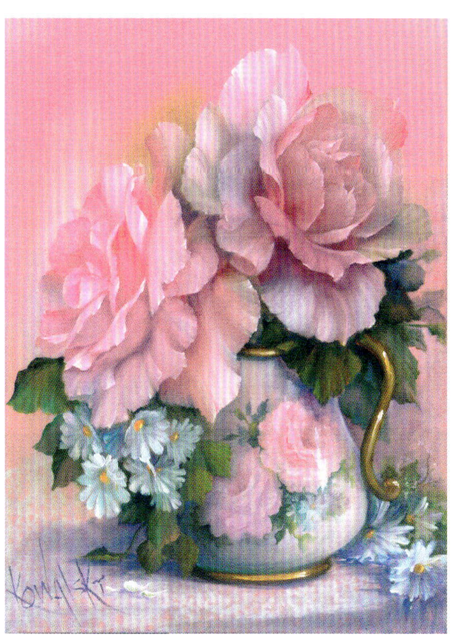

10. Add daisies to complete your painting. *Refer to How to Paint a Daisy in the Basic How-To Photographs.* Sign your masterpiece with pride!

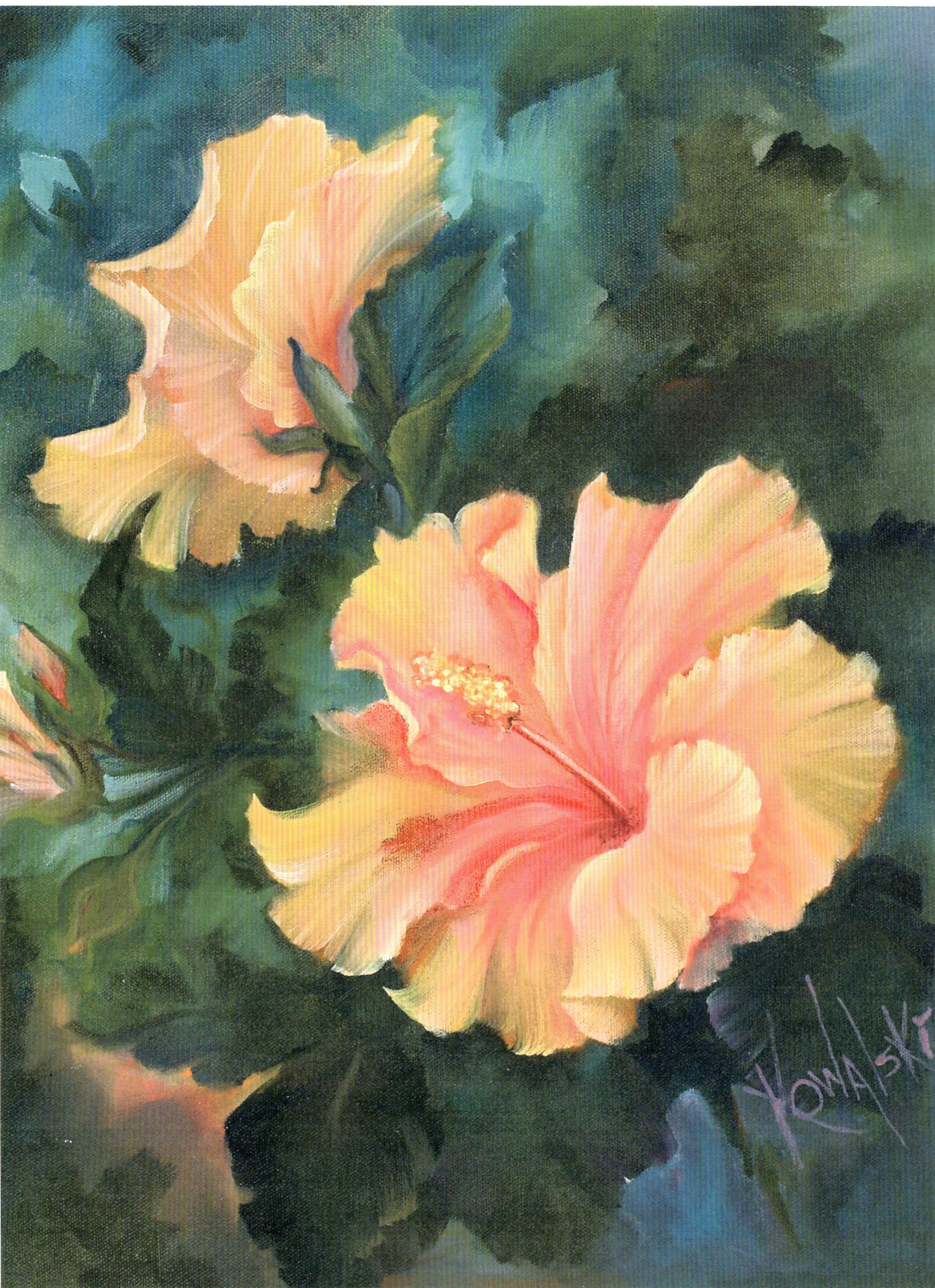
Kowalski

5. Tropical Hibiscus

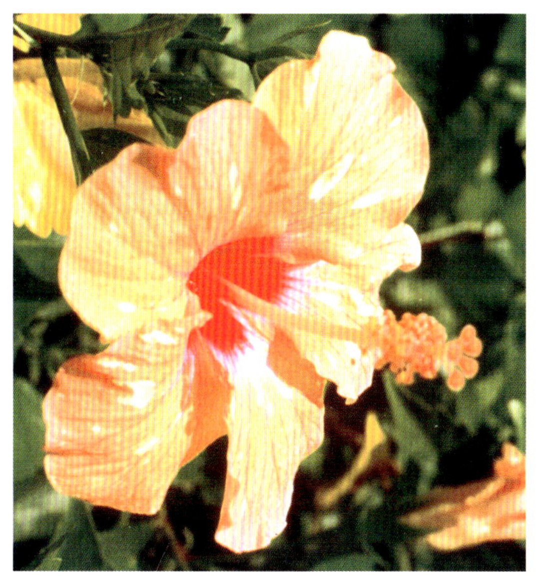

Use your photos as a jumping off point. Add half-open flowers and buds to a picture of a single hibiscus to create a more complex composition. And don't forget, hibiscus come in many colors -- White, Pink and Red are just a few.

Materials:

Bob Ross Soft Oil Colors:
Alizarin Crimson
Cadmium Yellow Light
Cadmium Orange
Flower Pink
Mauve
Sap Green
Titanium White
Turquoise
Ultramarine Blue

Bob Ross Mediums:
Bob Ross Oil Paint Medium
Bob Ross Odorless Thinner
Liquid Opal

Bob Ross Brushes:
1" Landscape Brush
3/4" Floral Brush
1/2" Floral Brush
Floral Filbert Brush
Small Round Floral Brush
Floral Fan Brush
#2 Liner Brush

Other Materials:
Bob Ross Disposable Floral Palette
1 Canvas (18x24)

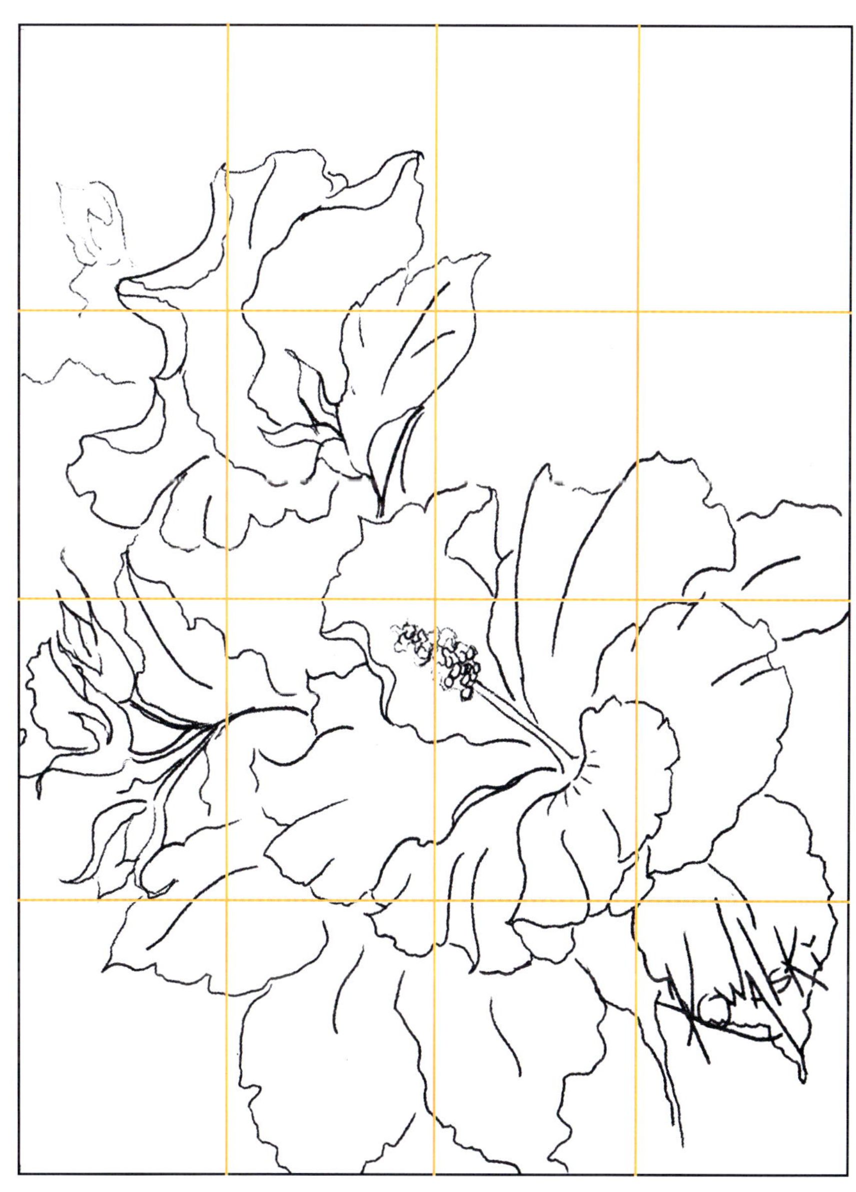

5. Tropical Hibiscus

Progressional Steps

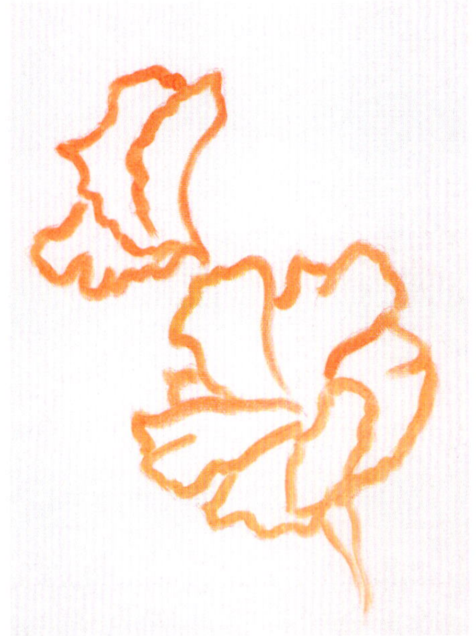

1. Start by using the small round brush to lightly sketch the hibiscus and bud with Flower Pink which has been thinned with Oil Paint Medium. Use the 1" brush to cover the background with a small amount of Liquid Opal.

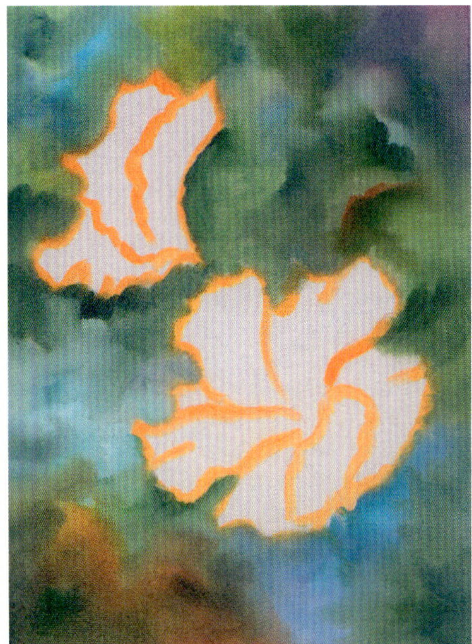

2. Then, add the background with various mixtures of Blue, Green, White, Turquoise, Yellow, Orange and Mauve. Use the fan brush to lightly blend and merge the background colors.

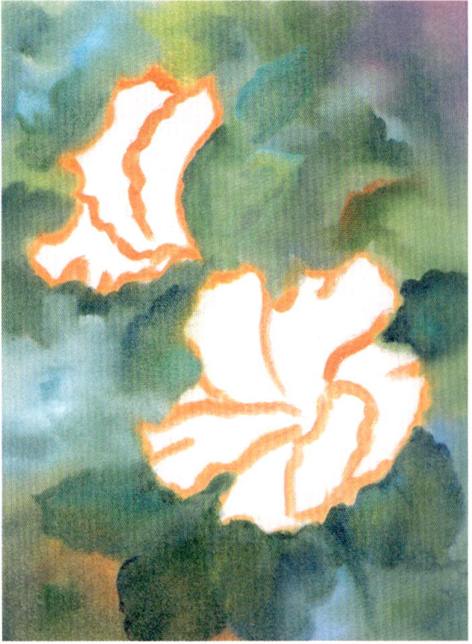

3. Loosely indicate the stem, leaves and diffused foliage with the 3/4" brush and various mixtures of Ultramarine Blue, Sap Green and Yellow and Orange, thinning the paint as necessary to keep it free-flowing.

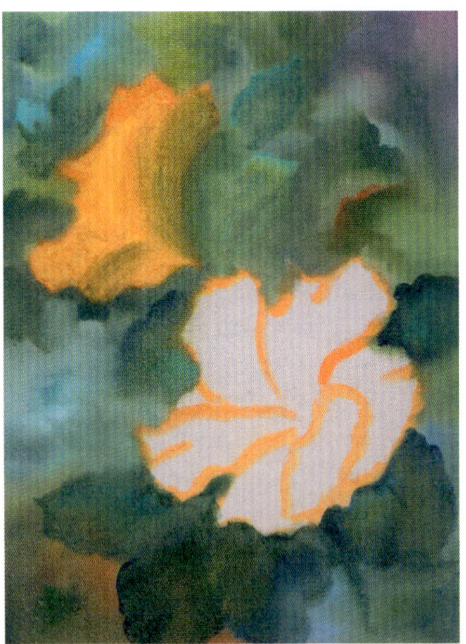

4. Loosely underpaint the large, half-open hibiscus bud with the 3/4" brush and thinned Orange and Yellow.

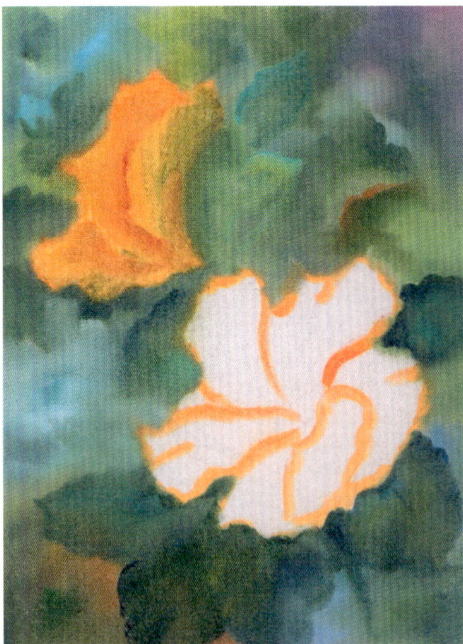

5. Add the dark shadowed areas of the bud with Alizarin Crimson and Flower Pink. Lightly blend and merge the shadows with a clean, dry brush.

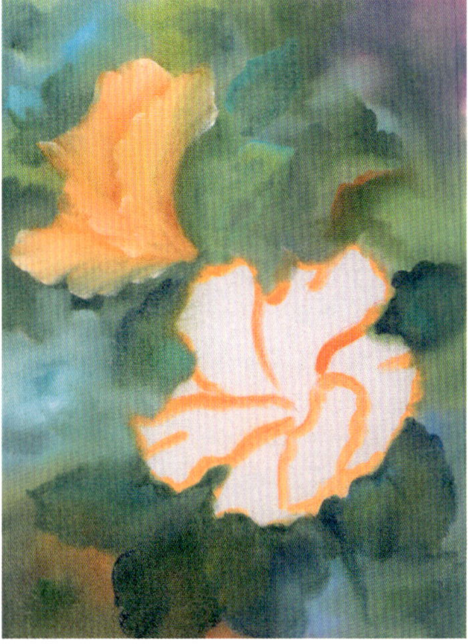

6. Highlight the bud with White and Yellow. Reloading the brush as necessary, start at the outside edge of each petal and direct a series of overlapping strokes towards the base of the bud. Be sure to thin the paint as necessary to insure, free-flowing strokes.

5. Tropical Hibiscus

Progressional Steps

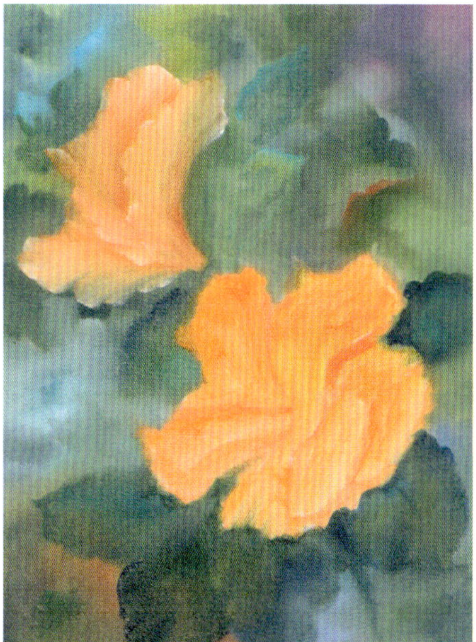

7. Underpaint the large flower with the 3/4" brush and a thinned mixture of Yellow and Orange.

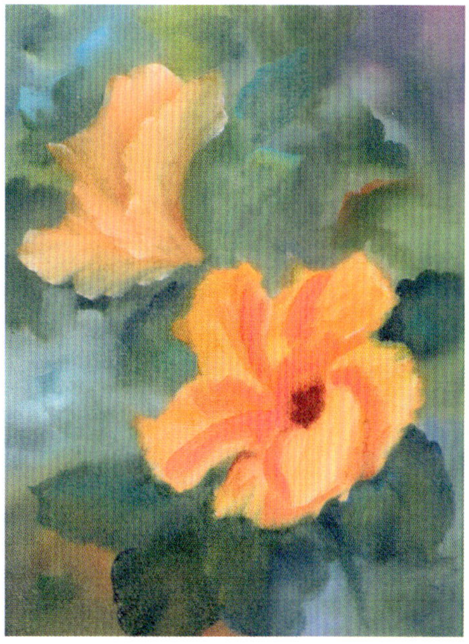

8. Add the shadowed areas with Alizarin Crimson and Flower Pink. Use the shadows to carefully create five petals.

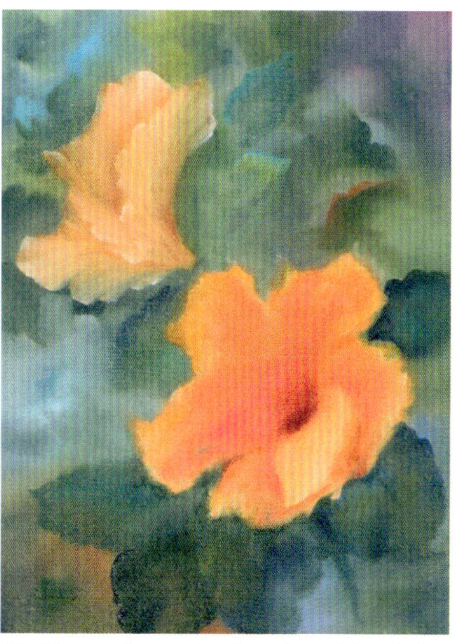

9. Use a clean, dry brush to blend the shadows into the base color of the flower.

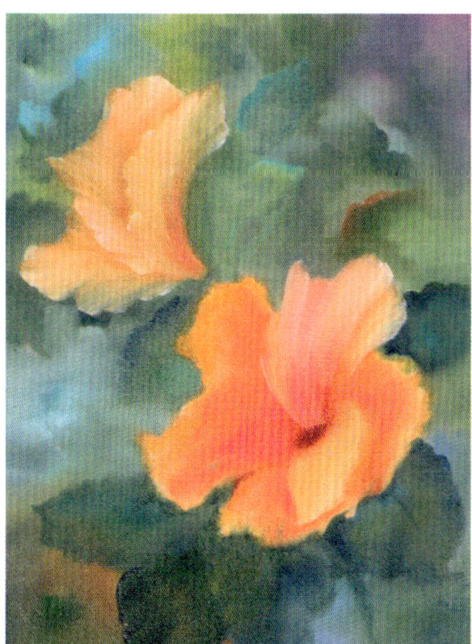

10. Highlight the petals with the 3/4" brush and White. Vary the color of the petals by tinting the White with small amounts of Flower Pink and Yellow. Carefully create individual petals...

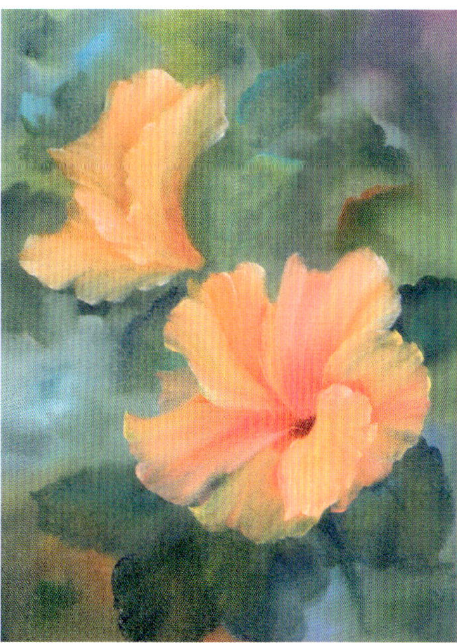

11. ...by starting at the outside edge of each petal and directing a series of overlapping strokes towards the center of the flower. Be sure to thin the paint as necessary to insure, long, smooth, silky, free-flowing strokes.

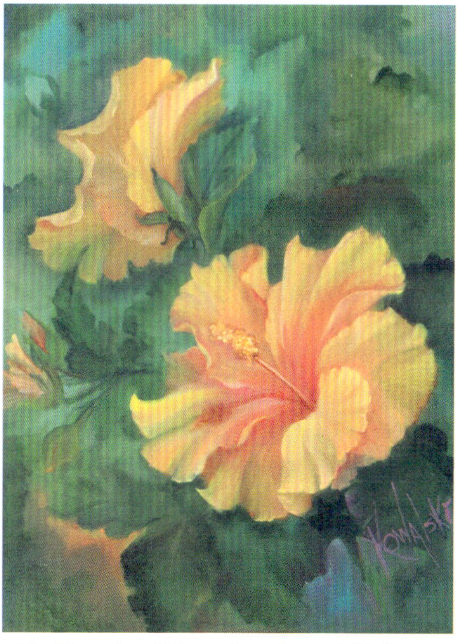

12. Use the filbert brush and Yellow, Orange and Pink to add small buds. Calyxes, small leaves and stems are thinned mixtures of Blue, Green and Yellow. The stamens are Alizarin Crimson and Yellow.

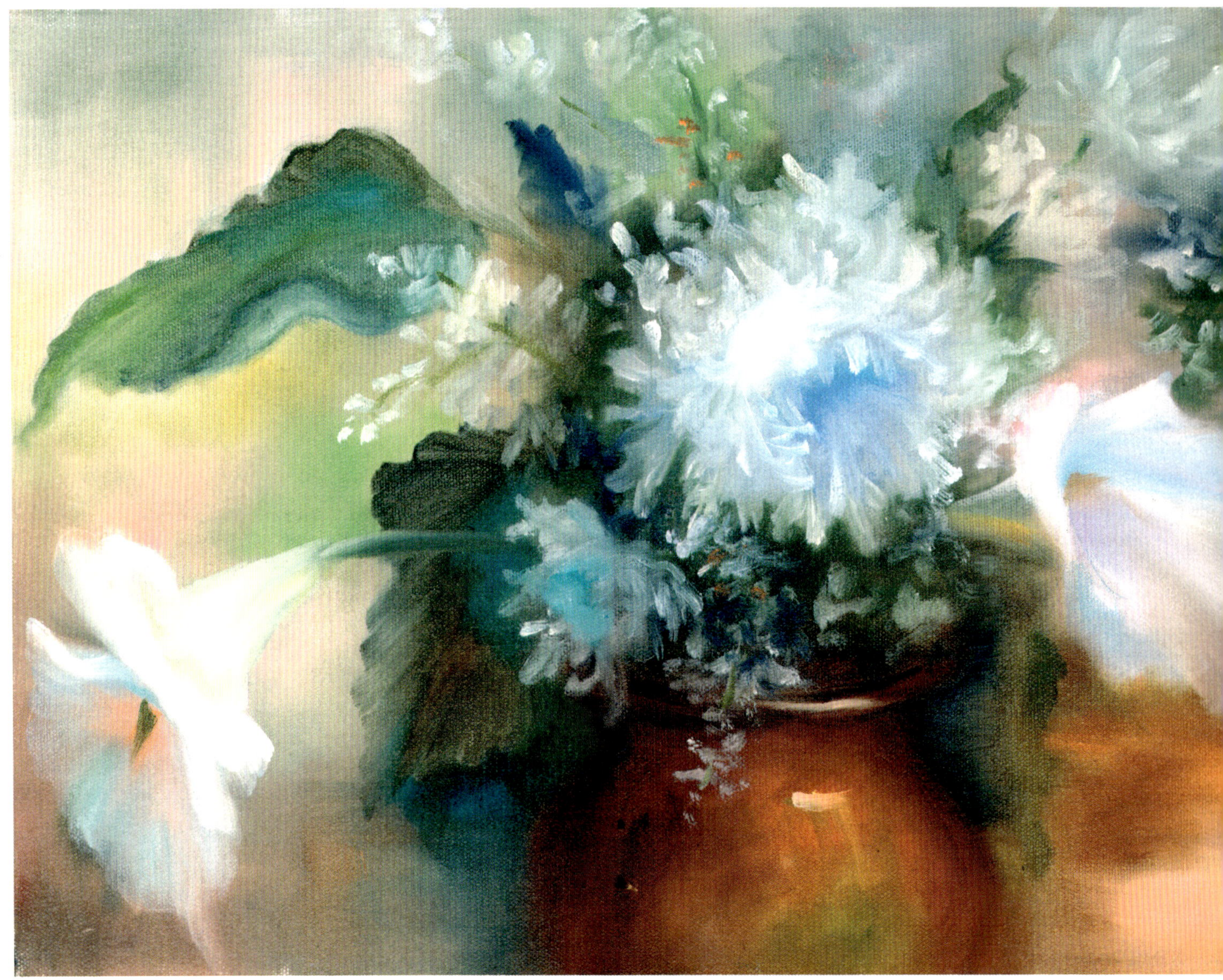

Materials:

Bob Ross Soft Oil Colors:
Alizarin Crimson
Cadmium Yellow Light
Cadmium Orange
Flower Pink
Mauve
Sap Green
Titanium White
Turquoise
Ultramarine Blue

Bob Ross Mediums:
Bob Ross Oil Paint Medium
Bob Ross Odorless Thinner
Liquid Opal

Bob Ross Brushes:
1" Landscape Brush
3/4" Floral Brush
1/2" Floral Brush
Floral Filbert Brush
Small Round Floral Brush
#2 Liner Brush

Other Materials:
Bob Ross Disposable Floral Palette
1 Canvas (12x24)

6. Lilies and Mums

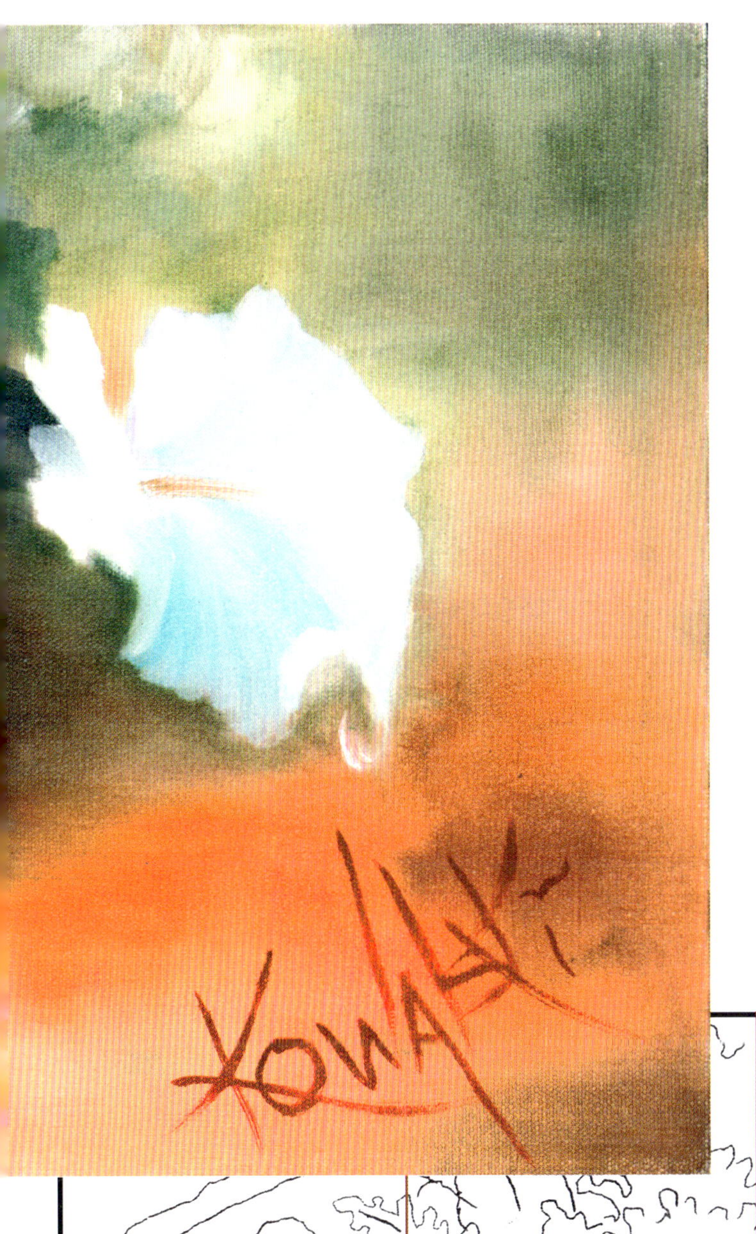

A very loose, impressionistic painting with few structured brush strokes. Calla lilies, tall willowy, majestic flowers on a short, horizontal canvas create an unexpected surprise. Replace these lilies with other tall flowers, such as sunflowers or irises.

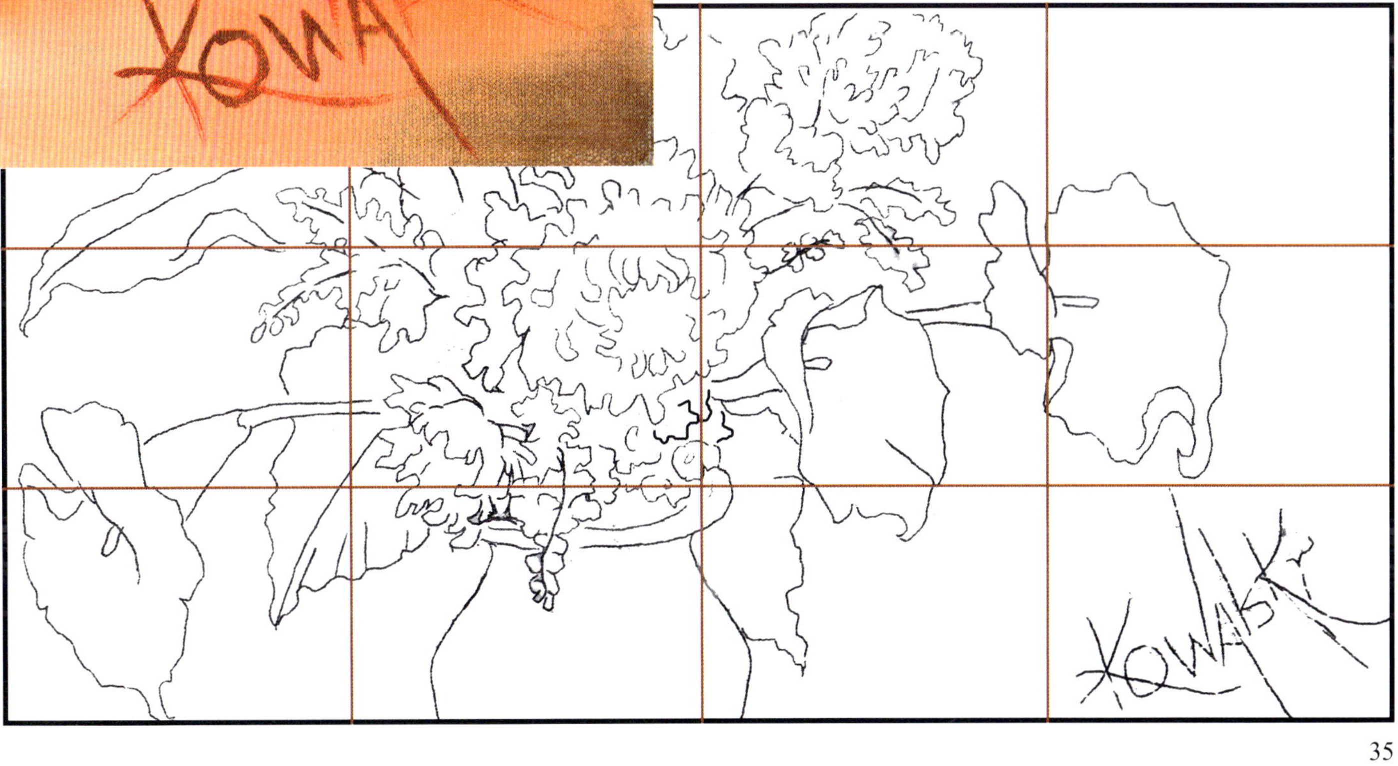

6. Lilies and Mums

Progressional Steps

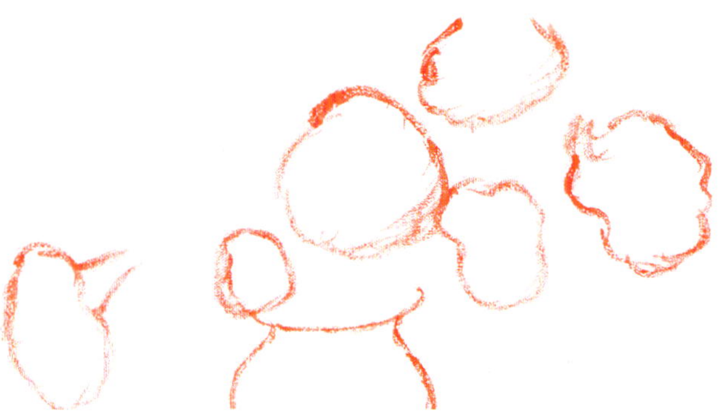

1. With thinned Orange on the small round brush, loosely sketch the placement of the pot, lilies and mums. Carefully avoiding the flowers and pot...

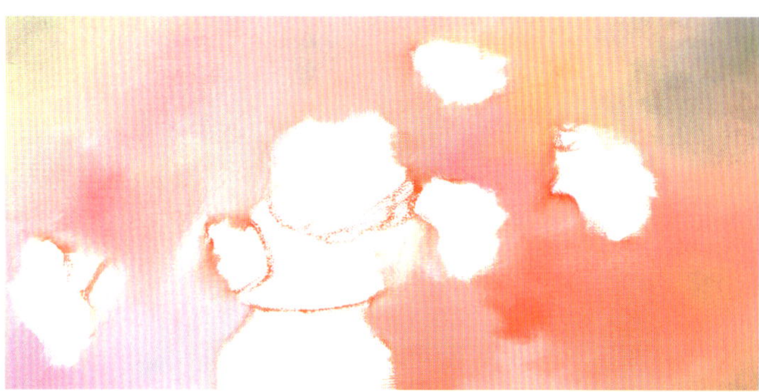

2. ...use the 1" brush to cover the canvas with Liquid Opal, then add various mixtures of Green, Blue, Orange, Pink, Yellow and Mauve to the background.

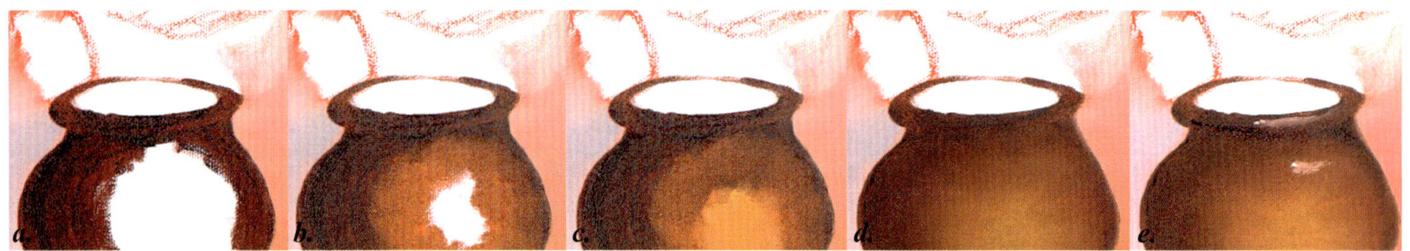

3. Painting the Ceramic Pot

Start by making a Brown mixture on your palette with equal parts of Alizarin Crimson and Sap Green.

a. Use the 3/4" brush to paint the dark, left side of the pot with the Brown mixture.

b. Add Orange to the Brown mixture and use loose, criss-cross strokes to paint the middle value of the pot.

c. Add Yellow to the Brown/Orange mixture to add the light value and to indicate the lip of the pot.

d. With the fan brush and sweeping horizontal strokes, very lightly blend the entire pot.

e. Final highlights are White.

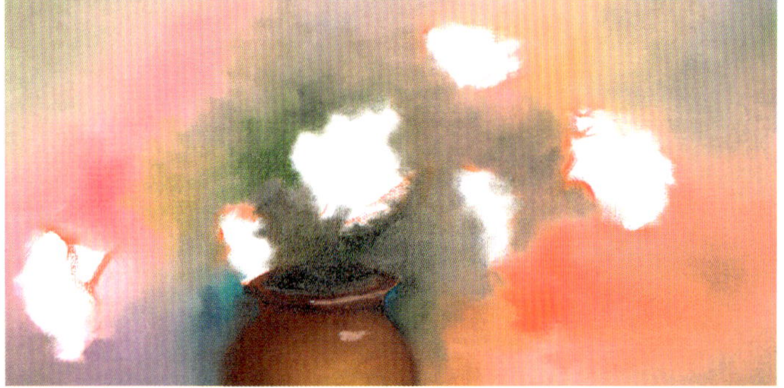

4. Use the 1/2" brush and loose strokes to block in the dark foliage areas with Green, Blue and Turquoise.

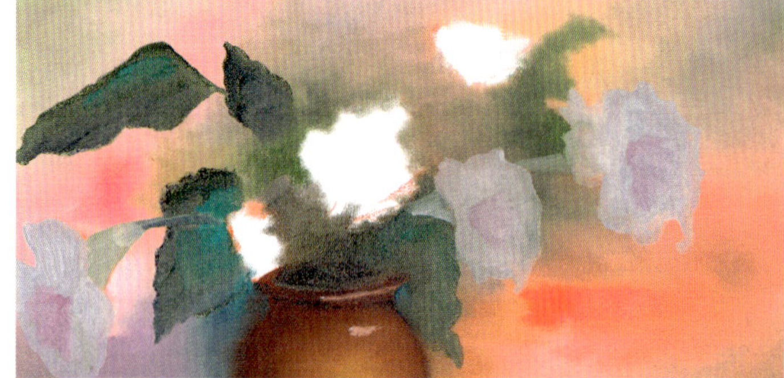

5. Add the large leaves with various mixtures of Blue and Green.

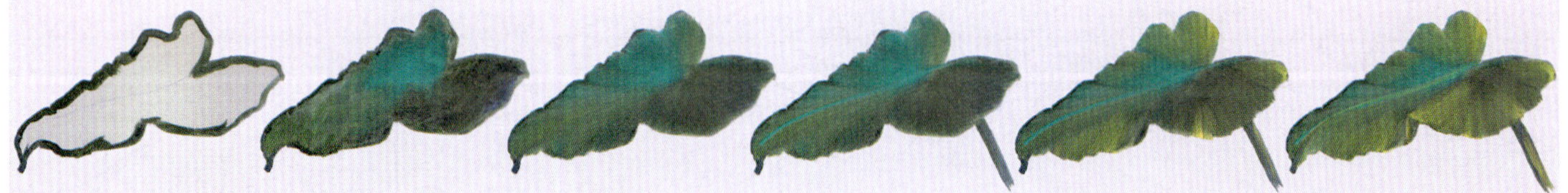

6. Painting Calla Lily Leaves

Loosely sketch each leaf. Underpaint with mixtures of Blue, Green and Turquoise. Highlight with Yellow.

6. Lilies and Mums

Progressional Steps

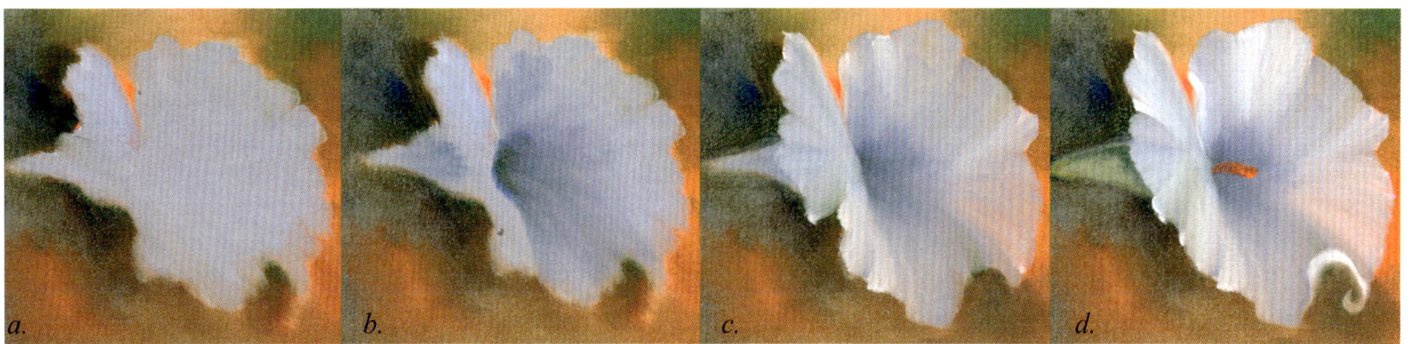

7. Painting the Calla Lilies

a. Use the 1/2" brush to loosely underpaint each lily with a mixture of White, Blue, Green and Mauve.
b. Add the dark, shadowed areas with Blue and Green.
c. Highlight the Lilies with White.
d. Finally add the stamen with a mixture of Orange and Alizarin Crimson - highlight with Yellow and Orange.

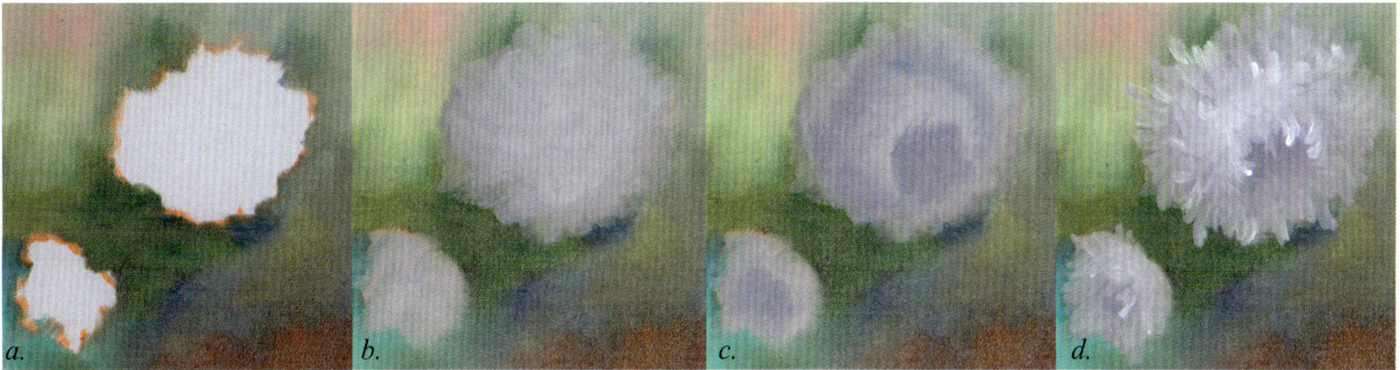

8. Painting the Mums

a. Loosely sketch each mum and bud.
*b.*Then, with various mixtures of White, Blue, Green and Mauve, loosely block in the mums.
c. Add the shadowed areas with Blue and Green.
d. Highlight with the filbert brush and White.

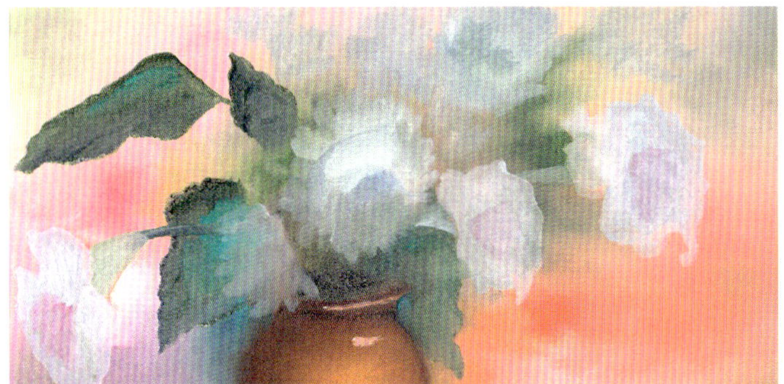

9. Add final highlights to the flowers and leaves...

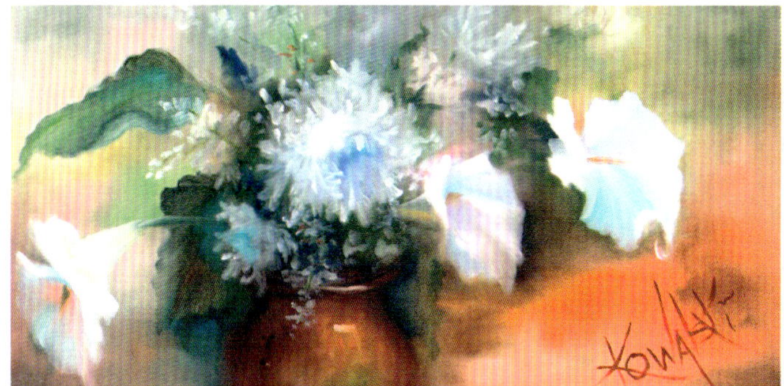

10. ... and the suggestion of tiny wildflowers with stems of Green and dots of White to complete your painting.

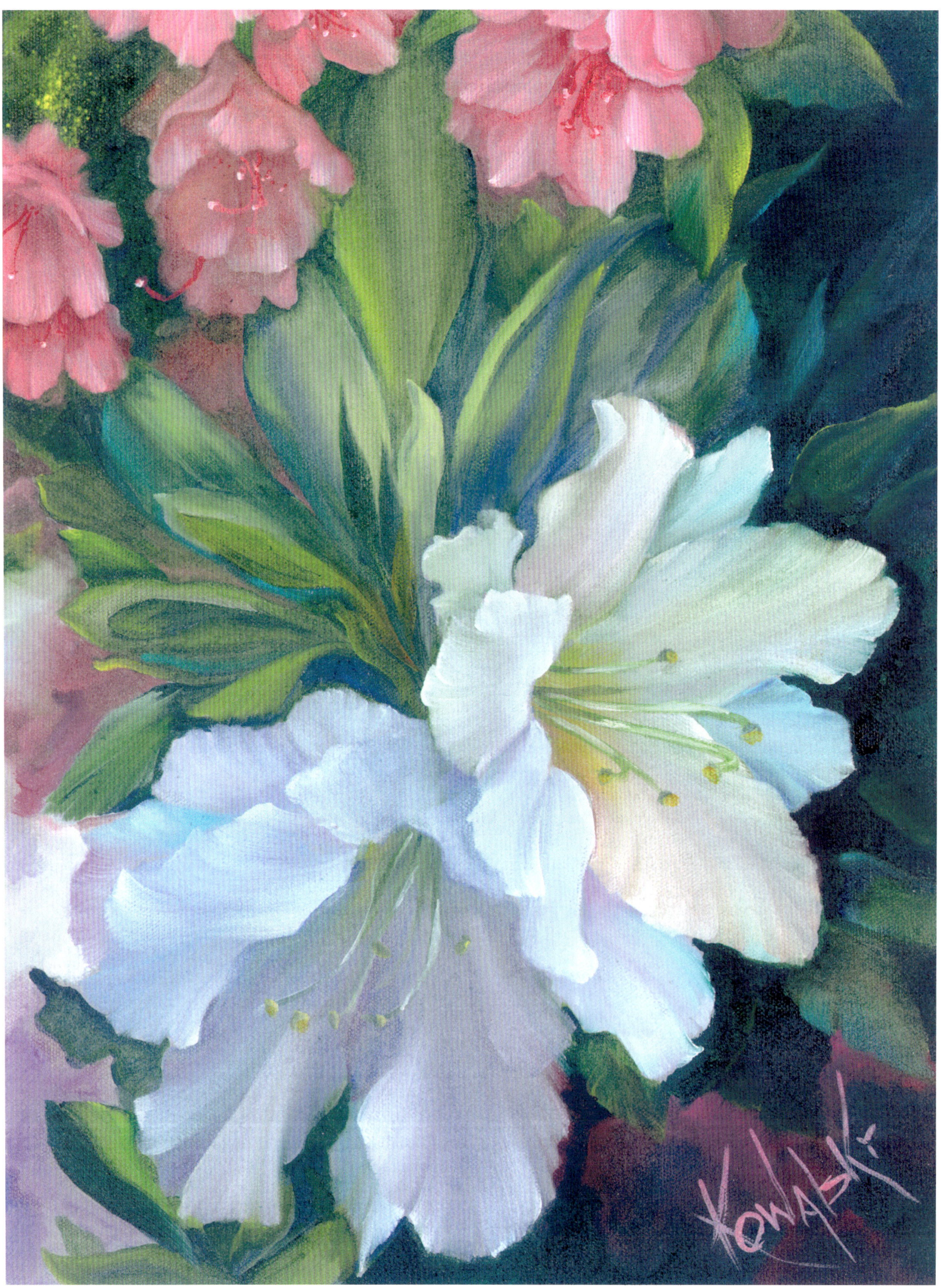

7. Pink and White Azaleas

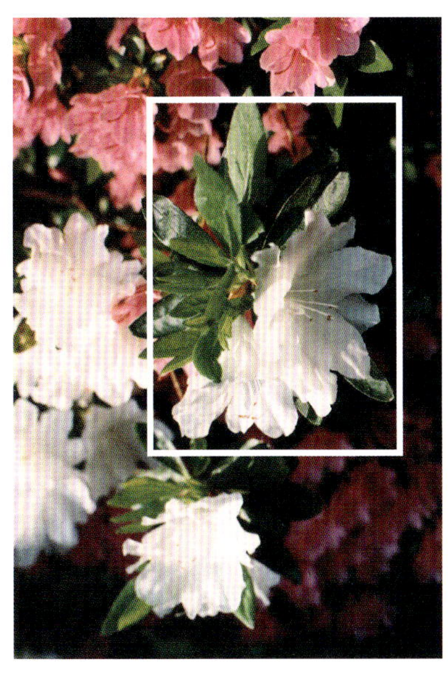

Try creating your next masterpiece from just a portion of a photograph. The result can be dramatic, large, oversized flowers.

Materials:

Bob Ross Soft Oil Colors:
Alizarin Crimson
Cadmium Yellow Light
Cadmium Orange
Dusty Rose
Flower Pink
Mauve
Sap Green
Titanium White
Turquoise
Ultramarine Blue

Bob Ross Mediums:
Bob Ross Oil Paint Medium
Bob Ross Odorless Thinner
Gray Gesso

Bob Ross Brushes:
1" Landscape Brush
3/4" Floral Brush
1/2" Floral Brush
Floral Filbert Brush
Small Round Floral Brush
#2 Liner Brush

Other Materials:
Bob Ross Disposable Floral Palette
1 Canvas (18x24)
Foam Applicator

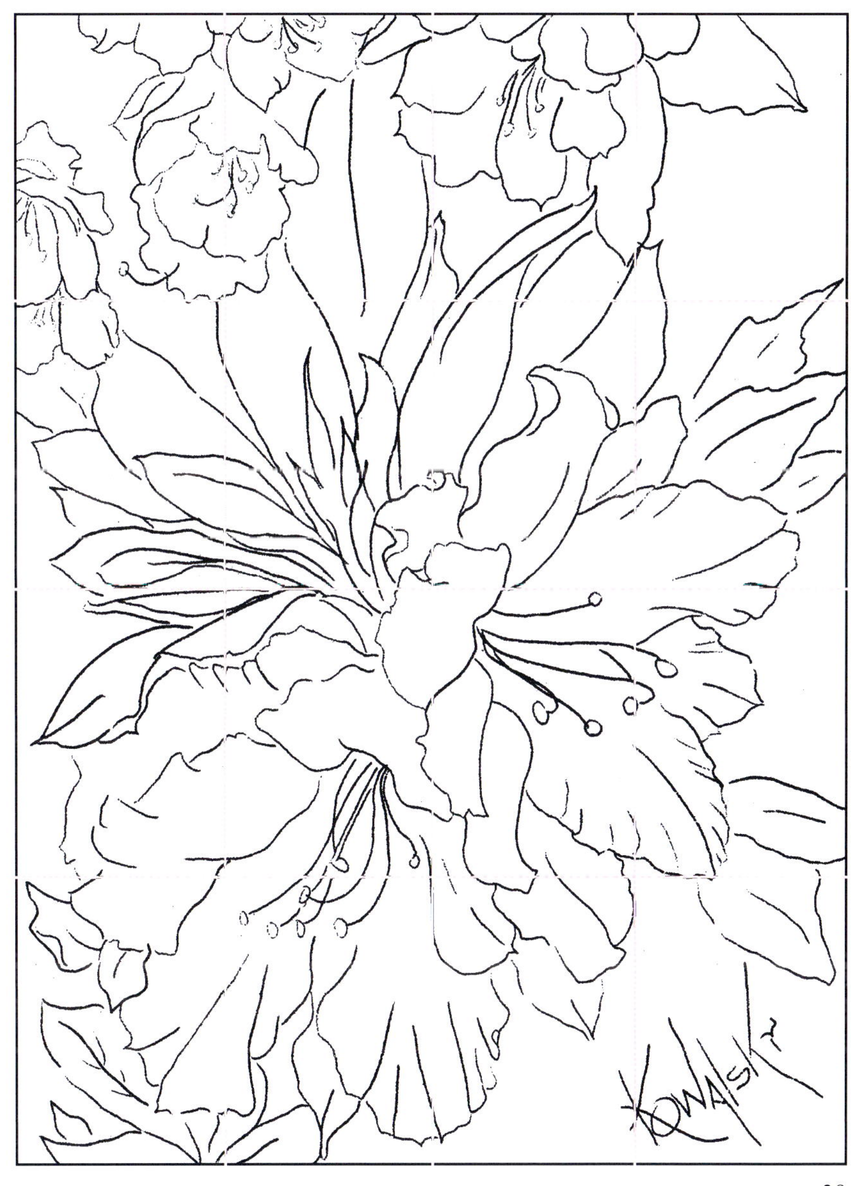

7. Pink and White Azaleas

Progressional Steps

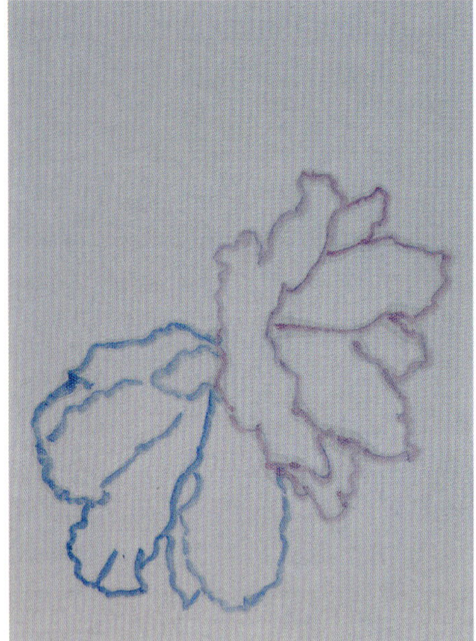

1. Start by using the foam applicator to cover the entire canvas with Gray Gesso and allow to dry completely. Use the small round brush and Blue to lightly sketch the placement of the two azaleas.

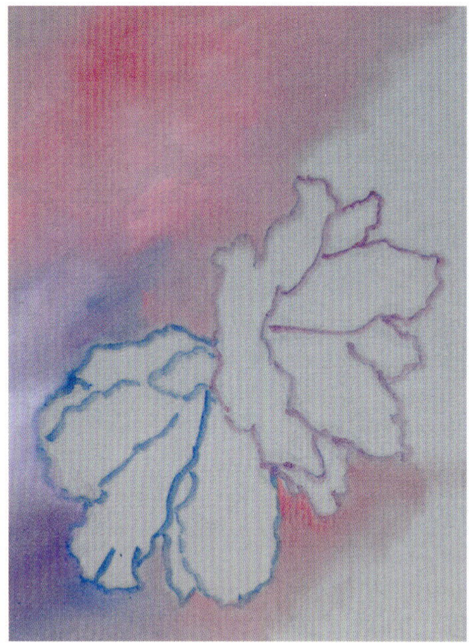

2. Use the 1" brush to cover the canvas with a very, very small amount of Oil Paint Medium. Then, add the background with various mixtures of Turquoise, Blue, Mauve, Pink and White.

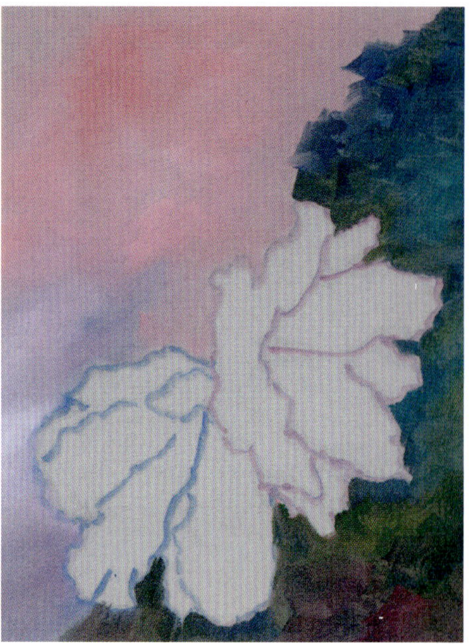

3. Loosely underpaint the foliage areas with various dark mixtures of Ultramarine Blue and Sap Green.

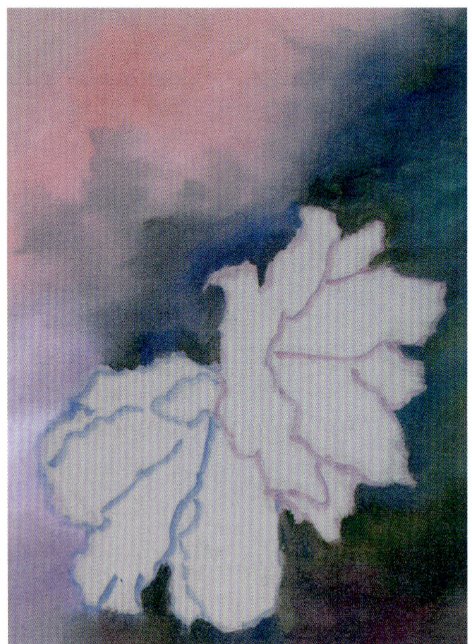

4. Use a clean, dry 1" brush to blend and merge the background colors.

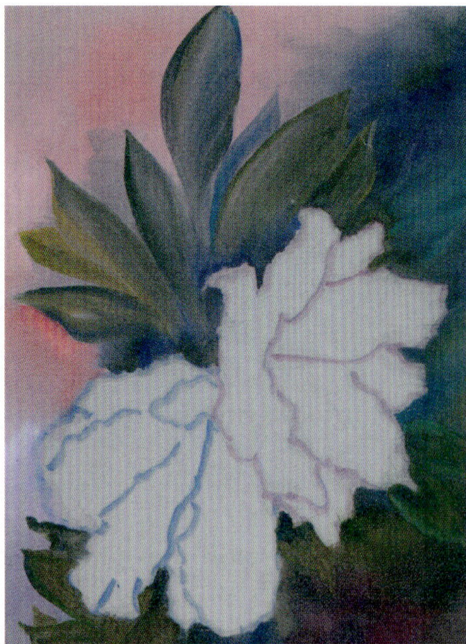

5. With the 3/4" brush, use various mixtures of Blue, Green, Turquoise, Yellow and White to add the large azalea leaves. If desired, use the 1/2" brush to paint the smaller leaves.

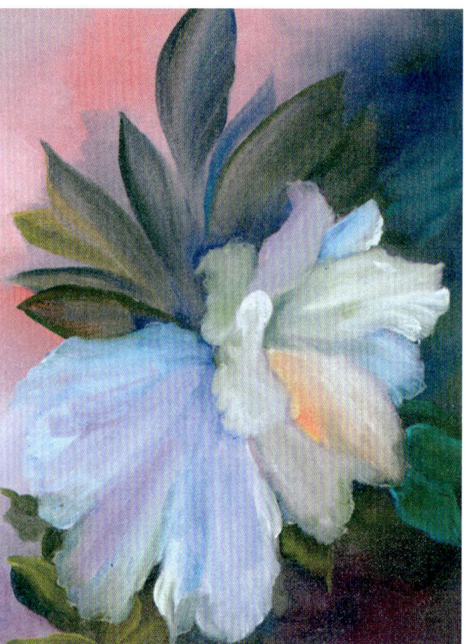

6. Underpaint the large azalea blossoms with the 3/4" brush and thinned White which has been tinted with various mixtures of Mauve, Blue, Green and Orange.

7. Pink and White Azaleas

Progressional Steps

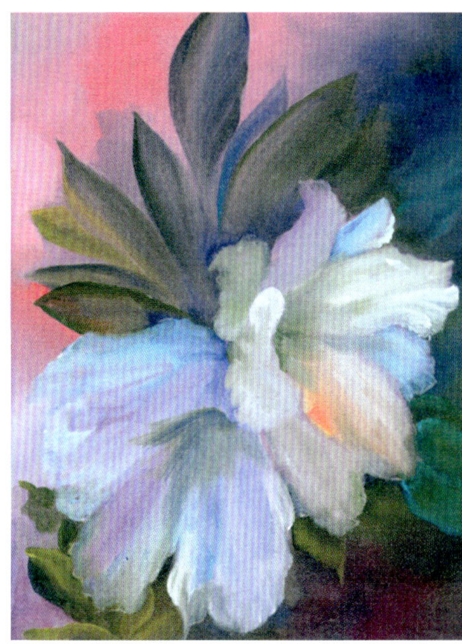

7. Highlight the azalea petals with the 3/4" brush and White which has been thinned with Medium and tinted with small amounts of Mauve, Green, Blue, Turquoise and Orange. Carefully create individual petals...

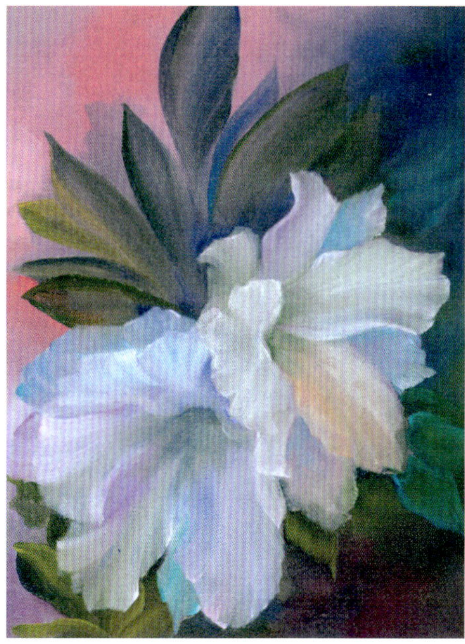

8. ...by loading the brush to a chiseled edge, starting at the outside edge of each petal and directing a series of overlapping strokes towards the center of the flower. Be sure to thin the paint as necessary...

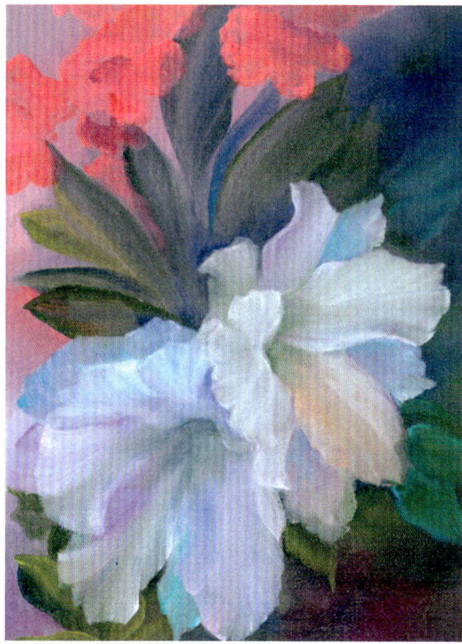

9. ... to insure, long, smooth, silky, free-flowing strokes. Add the small pink azaleas with the 1/2" brush and thinned Dusty Rose. Use mixtures of Alizarin Crimson and Mauve for the dark centers of the small flowers.

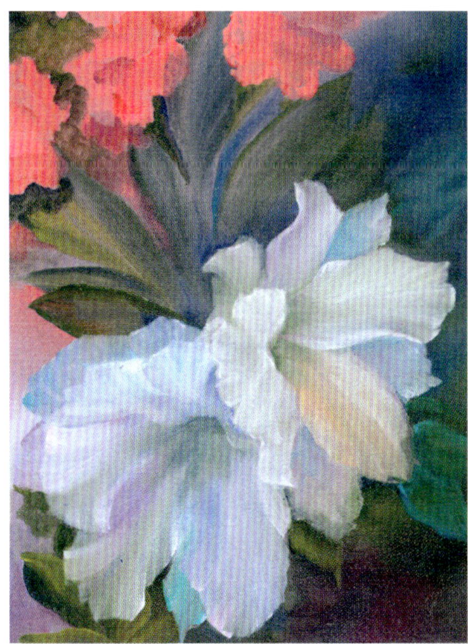

10. Indicate the small azalea foliage with mixtures of Blue and Green.

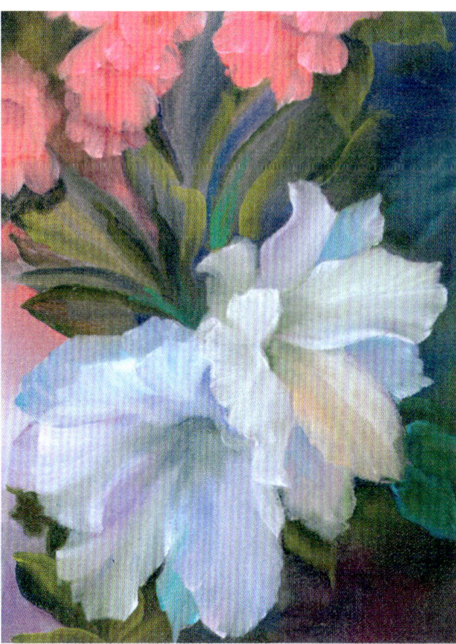

11. Highlight the small pink azaleas with the filbert brush and White. Then, add the tiny stamens with thinned Crimson and the liner brush.

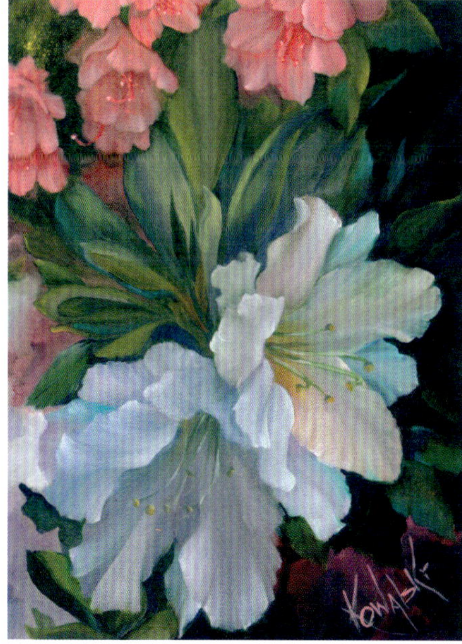

12. The stamens in the large white azaleas are added with the filbert brush and Green, Blue and White. Use Yellow and Orange to add stamen dots and additional highlights to the leaves. With the liner brush, sign with pride!

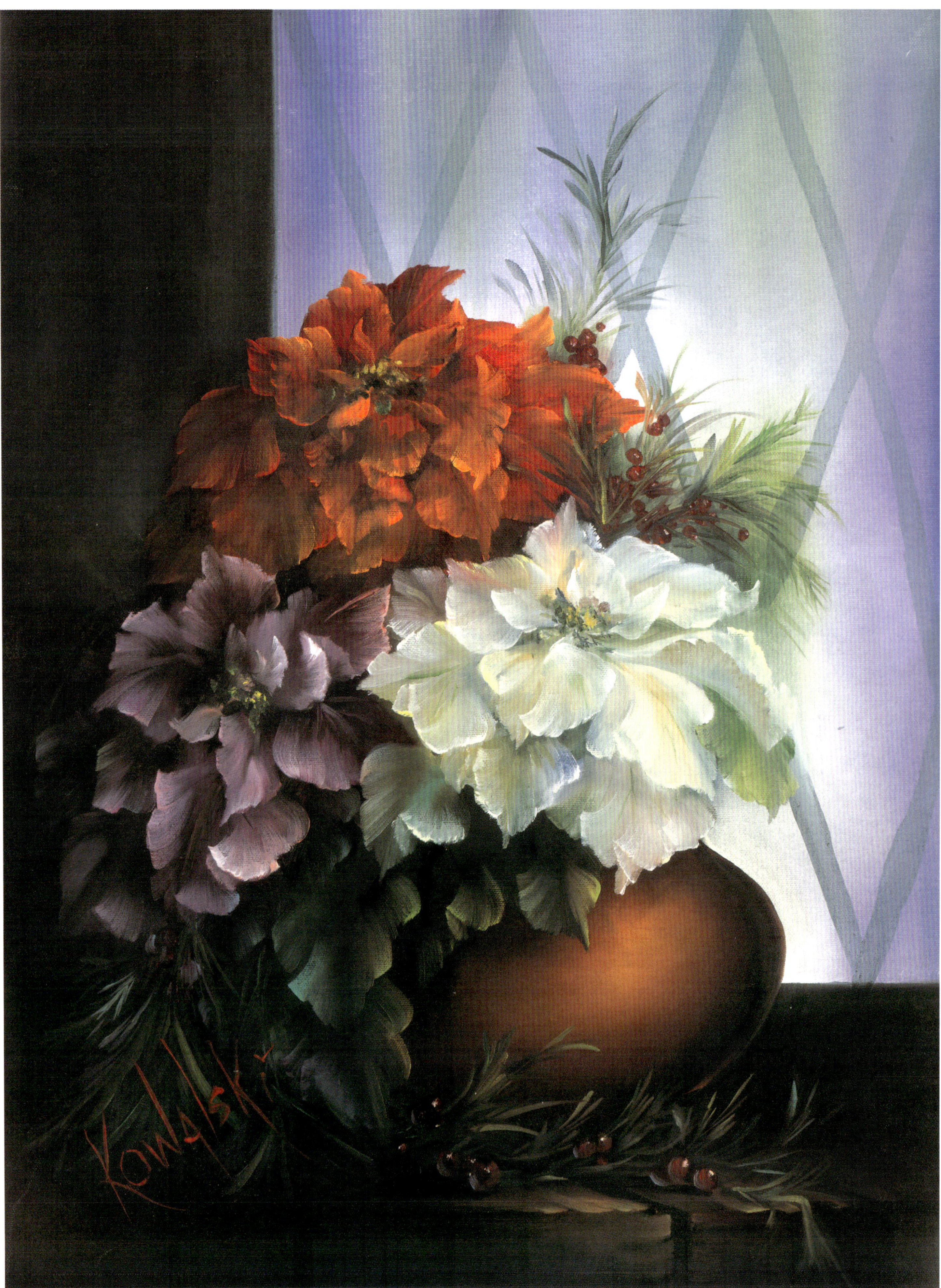
Kowalski

8. Poinsettias in a Window

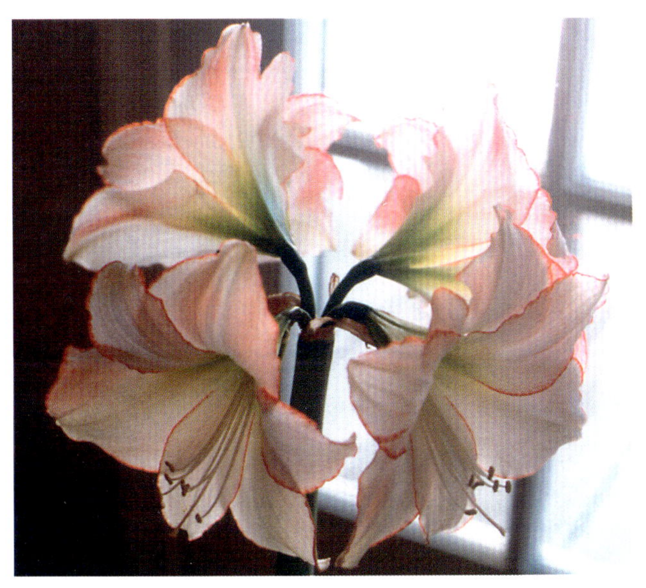

Back lighting from a window makes for a stunning floral composition. Try this painting idea with the Bob Ross Memorial Amaryllis for your next Christmas card.

Materials:

Bob Ross Soft Oil Colors:
Alizarin Crimson
Cadmium Yellow Light
Cadmium Orange
Cadmium Red Light
Cadmium Red Medium
Flower Pink
Mauve
Sap Green
Titanium White
Turquoise
Ultramarine Blue

Bob Ross Mediums:
Bob Ross Oil Paint Medium
Bob Ross Odorless Thinner
Black Gesso
Gray Gesso

Bob Ross Brushes:
1" Landscape Brush
3/4" Floral Brush
1/2" Floral Brush
Floral Filbert Brush
Small Round Floral Brush
#2 Liner Brush

Other Materials:
Bob Ross Disposable Floral Palette
1 Canvas (18x24)
Foam Applicator
Masking Tape

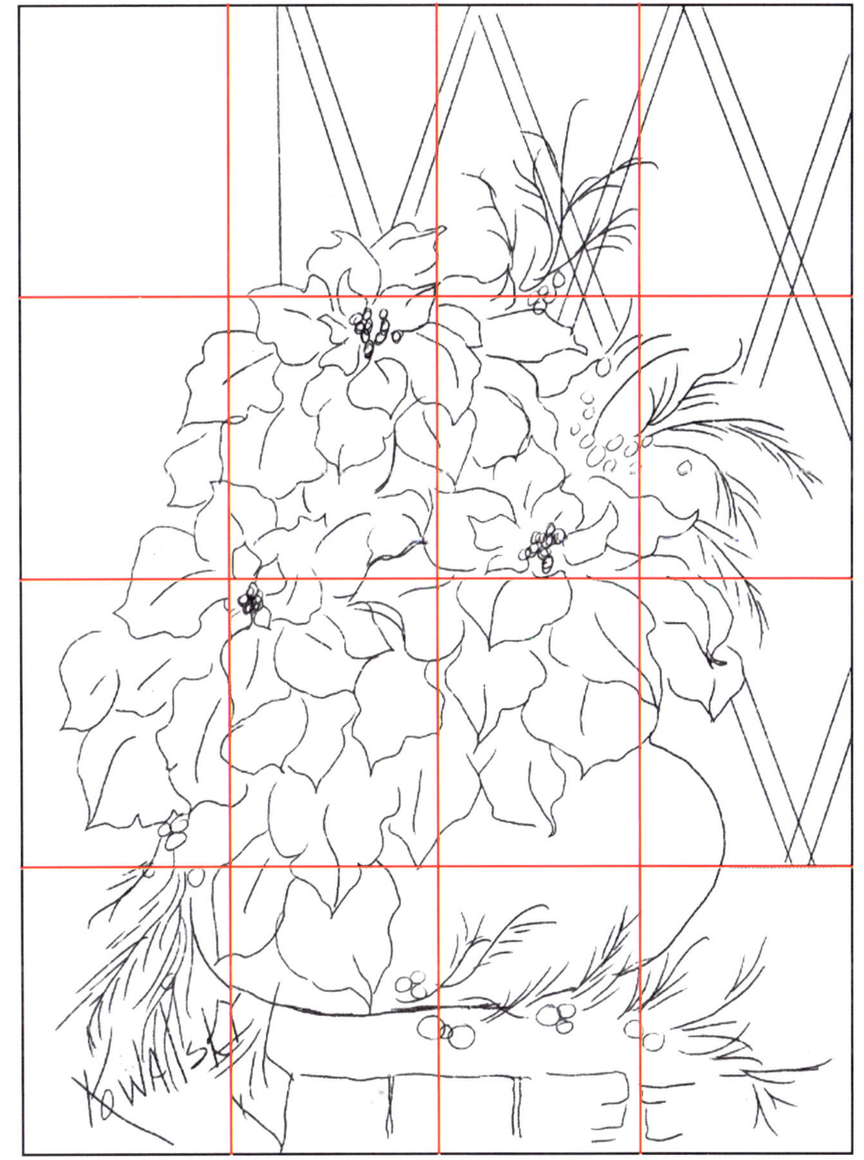

8. Poinsettias in a Window

Progressional Steps

Canvas Preparation
Use the foam applicator to cover the entire canvas with a thin, even coat of Gray gesso and allow to dry completely. When the Gray gesso is dry, use strips of masking tape to mask off a five-inch border on the left side of the canvas and a six-inch border across the bottom of the canvas. Use the foam applicator to apply a thin, even coat of Black gesso to these borders. Remove the strips of masking tape and continue using the foam applicator and Black gesso to underpaint the clay pot and to add the suggestion of window panes. Allow the canvas to dry completely before proceeding.

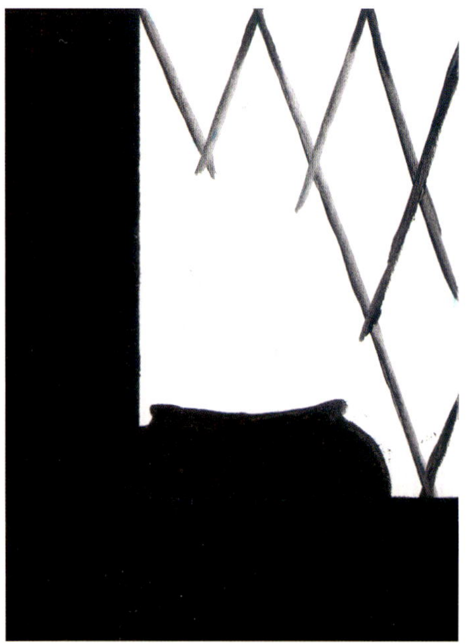

1. Prep the canvas with a foam applicator and Black and Gray Gesso. Allow the canvas to dry completely before proceeding.

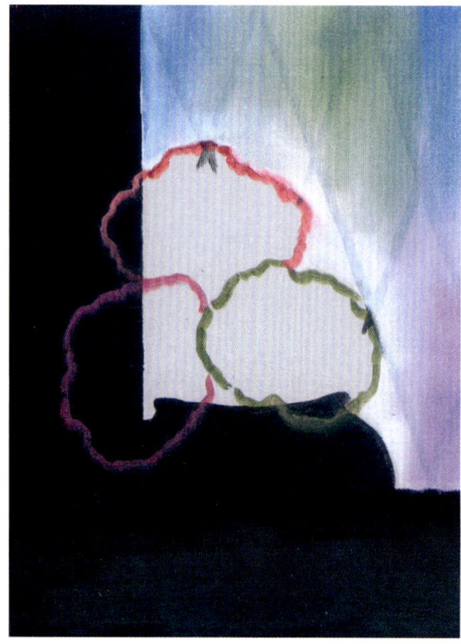

2. Then use Alizarin Crimson, Mauve and Green to sketch the flower placement. Avoiding the flowers, cover the entire canvas with a thin, even coat of Medium.

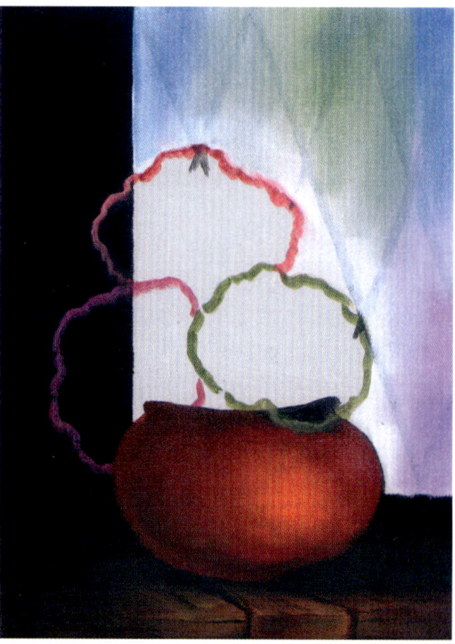

3. With the 1" brush, tint the window with various mixtures of White, Blue, Mauve and Green. Then, use the 3/4" brush to add the clay pot and table top.

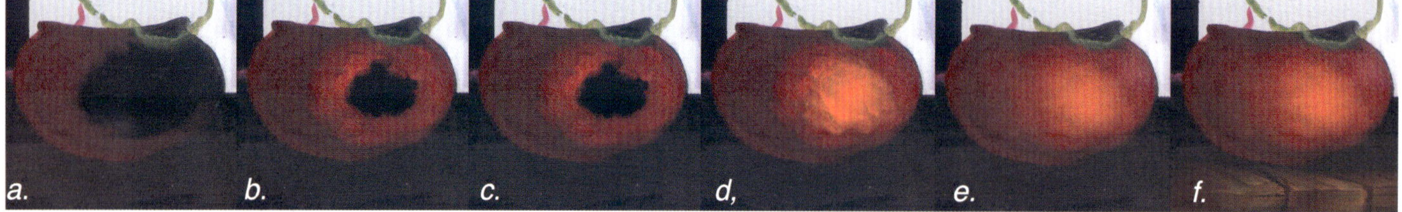

4. Painting the Clay Pot and Tabletop

Start by making a Brown mixture on your palette with equal parts of Alizarin Crimson and Sap Green.

a. Use the 3/4" brush to paint the dark, left side of the pot with the Brown mixture.
b. Add Red Medium to the Brown mixture and use loose, criss-cross strokes to paint the middle value of the pot.
c. Add Red Light to the Brown/Red mixture to add the light value.
d. With the fan brush and sweeping horizontal strokes, very lightly blend the entire pot.
e. Use a Mauve/Turquoise mixture for the reflected light on the left side of the pot. Blend lightly.
f. Indicate the table top with the light mixture and short horizontal strokes. Reflected light is Red Light.

8. Poinsettias in a Window

Progressional Steps

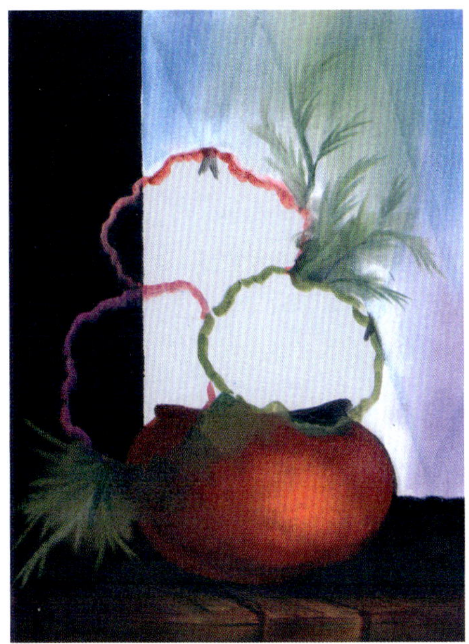

5. Block in dark foliage areas near the flowers with the 3/4" brush and a mixture of Green and Blue. Then use the chiseled edge of the brush to begin shaping ferns or pine needles near the flowers.

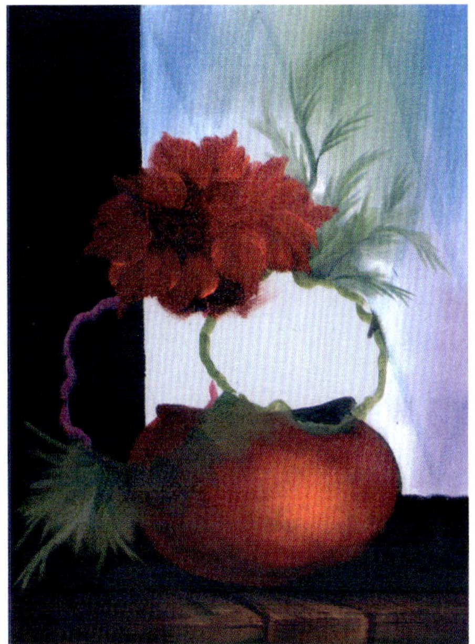

6. The Red poinsettia is underpainted with the 1/2" brush and Alizarin Crimson. (Keep in mind that the petals of the poinsettia are really leaves, and should be painted as such.) Complete each flower, one petal at a time.

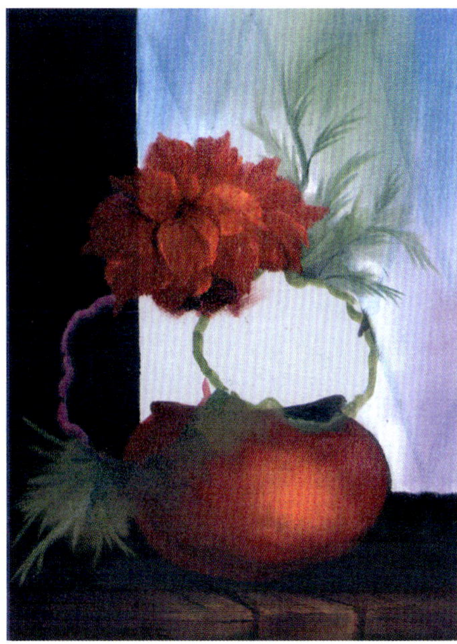

7. Highlight with Cadmium Red Medium, angling a series of overlapping strokes towards the center base of each petal. Use the chiseled edge of the brush to cut in the center vein of each petal.

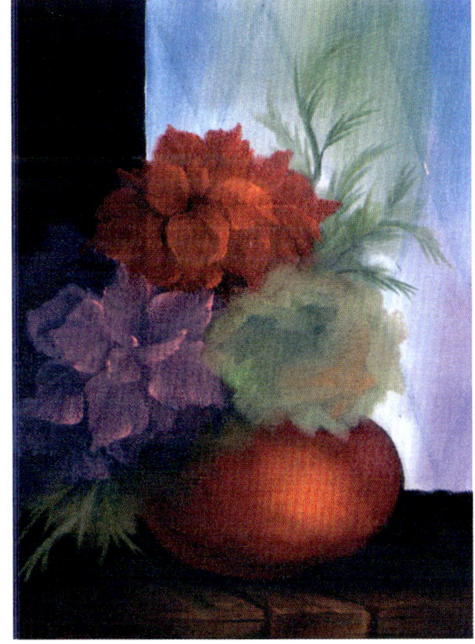

8. The Pink poinsettia is underpainted with thinned Mauve and highlighted with Flower Pink. Use a mixture of Flower Pink and Titanium White for highlights. Underpaint the White flower with White, Sap Green and Orange.

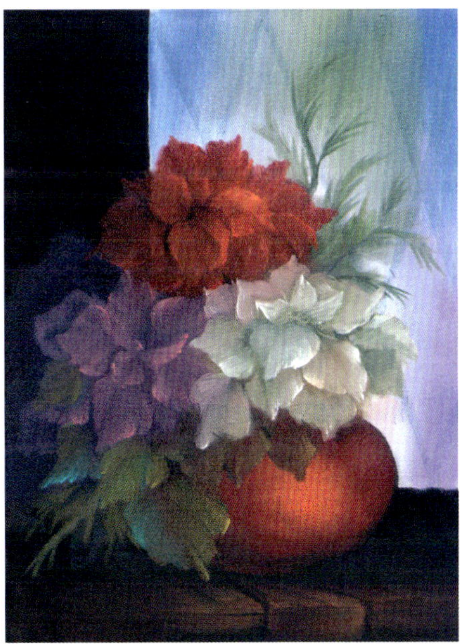

9. Highlight the White flower with White, which as been tinted with a small amount of Orange. Add the final leaves with Green and Blue - highlight with Yellow and Turquoise.

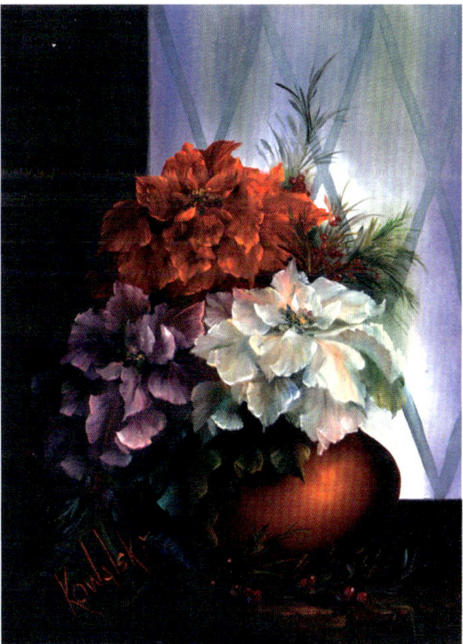

10. Use the filbert brush with a mixture of Orange and Green to push in the tiny leaf-buds in the centers of the flowers. Continue adding leaves, ferns and pine branches. Small Red berries are Cadmium Red Medium.

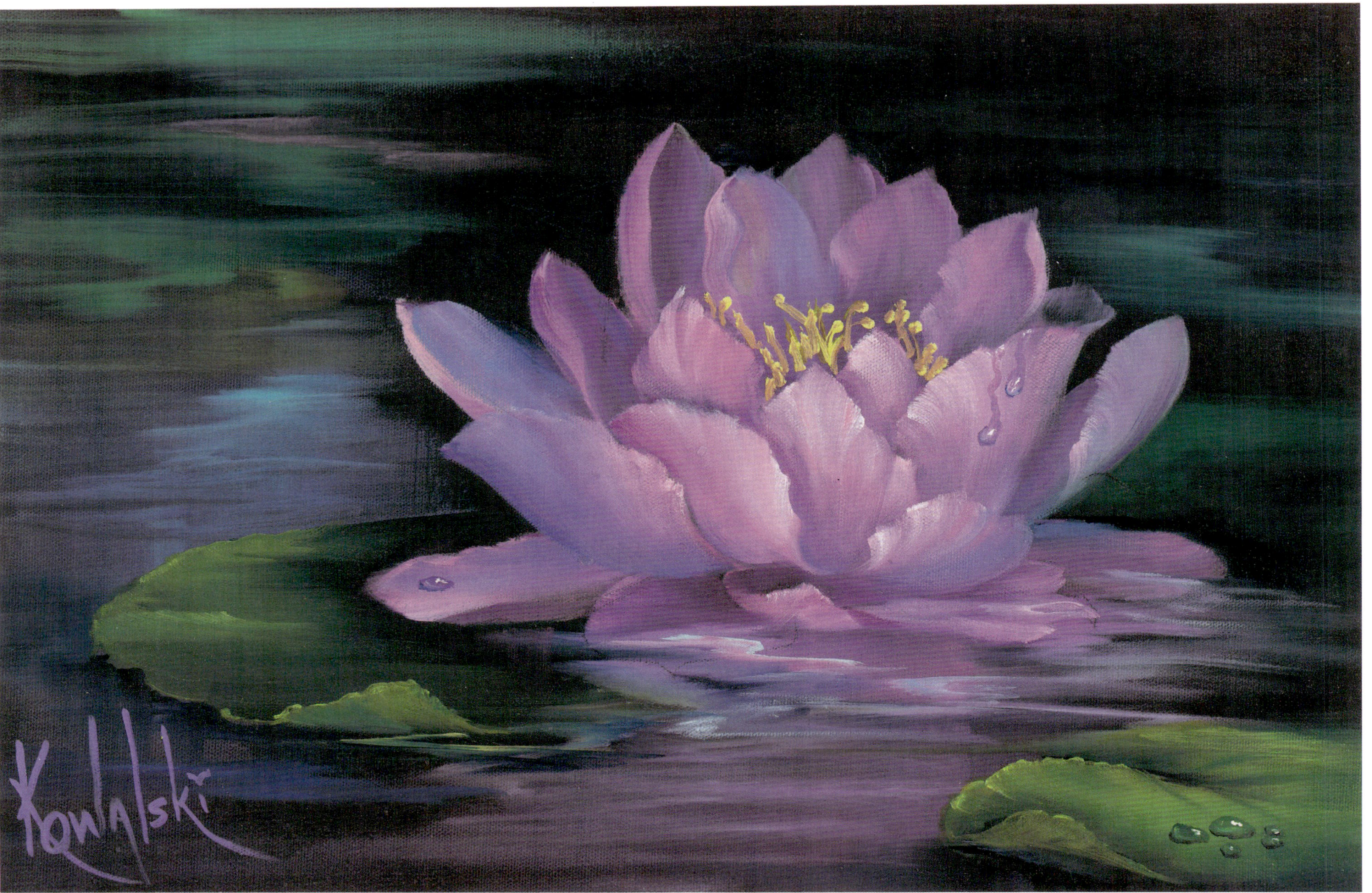
Kowalski

9. Magenta Waterlily

This painting is an excellent choice for a dramatic, twenty-four by thirty-six-inch canvas. Don't feel limited to Magenta - waterlilies come in many colors; White, Yellow and Pink are just a few. Why not two or more lilies and perhaps a dragon-fly? Create your own masterpiece and enjoy!

Materials

Bob Ross Soft Paints:
Cadmium Yellow
Magenta
Mauve
Sap Green
Titanium White
Turquoise
Ultramarine Blue

Bob Ross Mediums:
Black Gesso
Oil Paint Medium
Odorless Thinner

Bob Ross Brushes:
1" Landscape Brush
3/4" Floral Brush
Floral Round Brush
Liner Brush

Other Supplies:
Bob Ross Floral Palette
Foam Applicator
Canvas 18x24

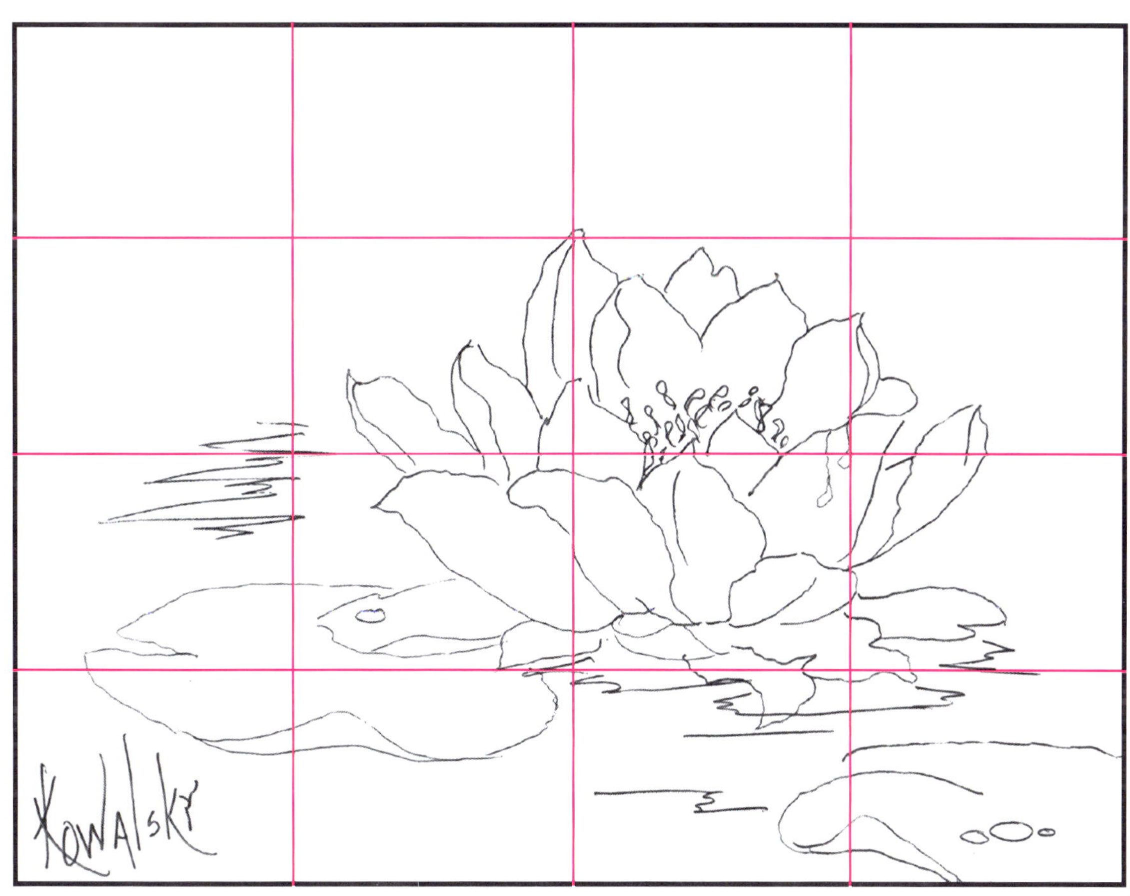

9. Magenta Waterlily

Progressional Steps

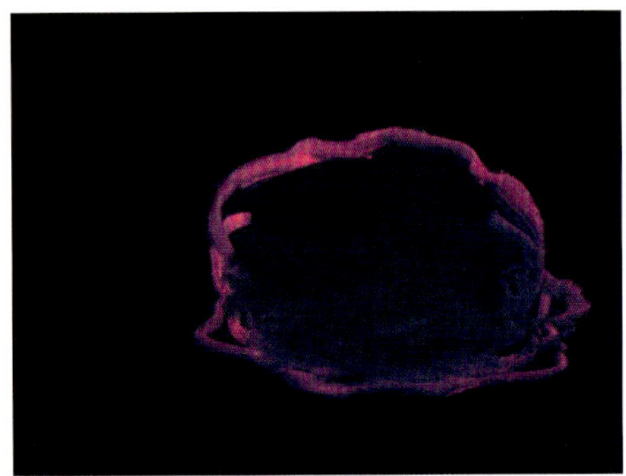

1. Use a foam applicator to cover the entire canvas with Black Gesso and allow to dry. Then use the small round brush with a mixture of Thinner and Magenta to loosely sketch the waterlily.

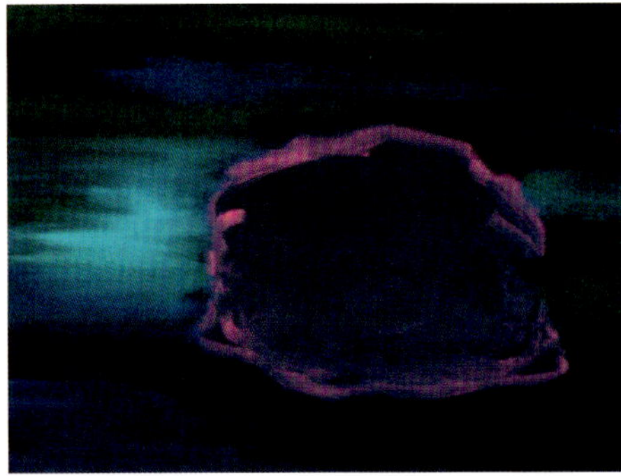

2. With the 1" brush, apply a very, very small amount of Medium to the canvas. Add various mixtures of Green, Blue, Mauve, Turquoise and Magenta to the background water.

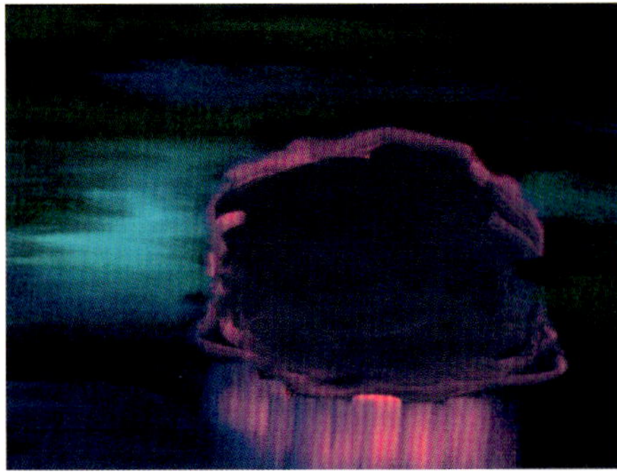

3. Use a clean, dry brush to blend the water with long, horizontal strokes. The flower will be Magenta, so reflect that color into the foreground water with vertical strokes...

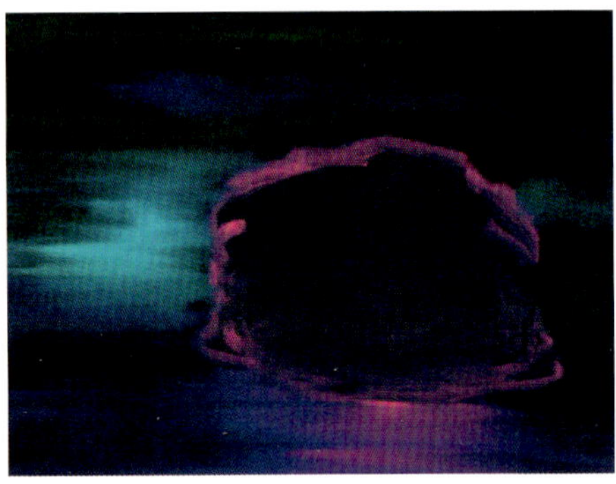

4. ...then lightly brush across with a clean, dry 1" brush and long, horizontal strokes.

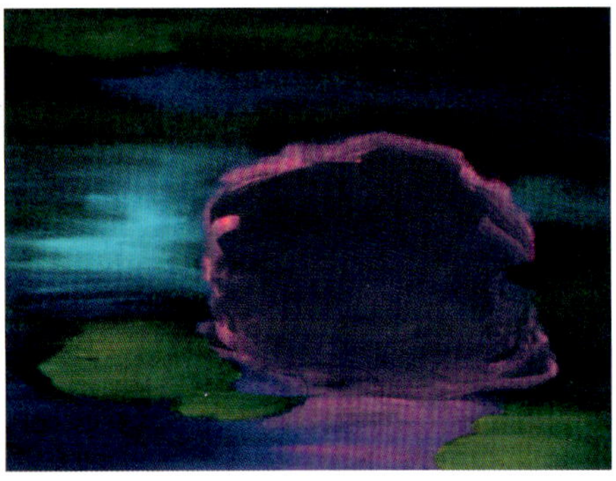

5. Use the 3/4" brush with mixtures of Blue and Green to add the indication of leaves. (The lily pads.)

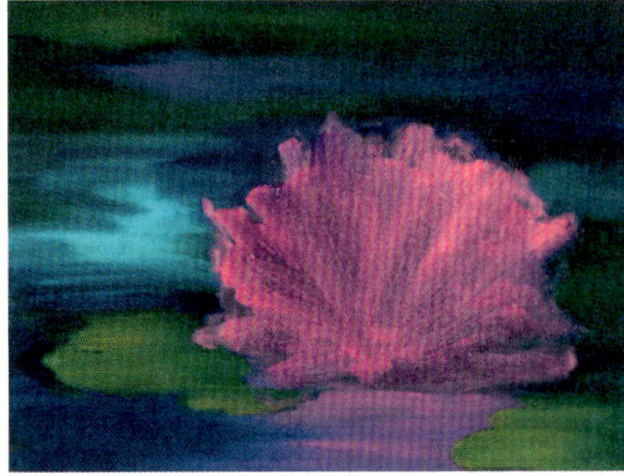

6. With a thin mixture of Magenta and Oil Paint Medium, use the 3/4" brush to underpaint the waterlily with loose strokes all directed towards the center of the flower.

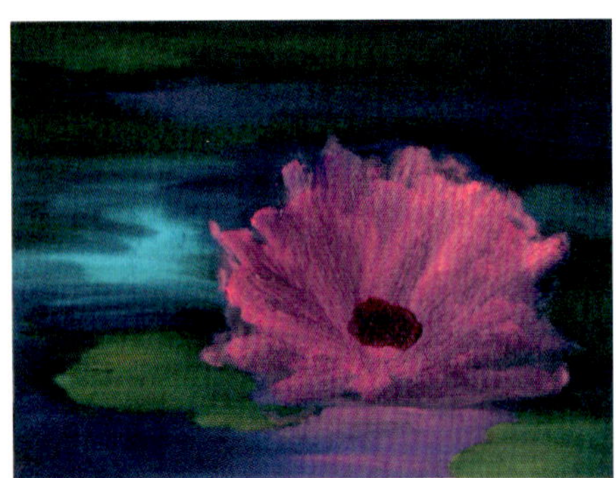

7. Add Mauve to the center of the flower............

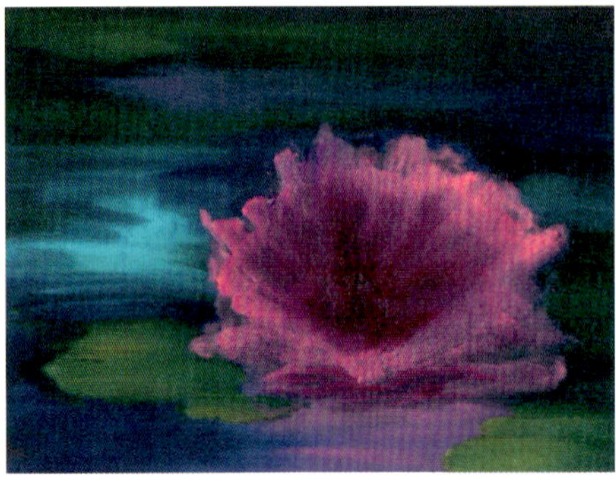

8. ...then blend the color out, towards the top of the lily.

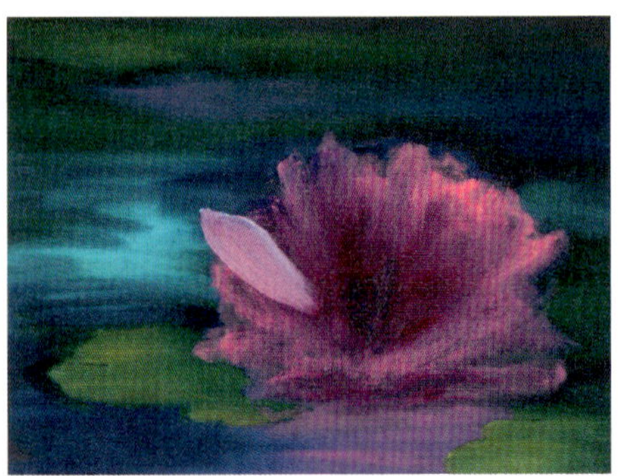

9. Use the 3/4" brush and various mixtures of Magenta, White and Turquoise to highlight the back petals.

9. Magenta Waterlily

Progressional Steps

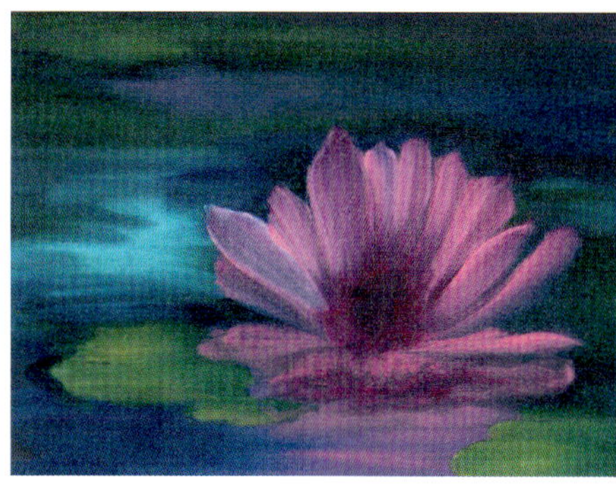

10. Use loose, overlapping strokes. all directed towards the center of the flower.

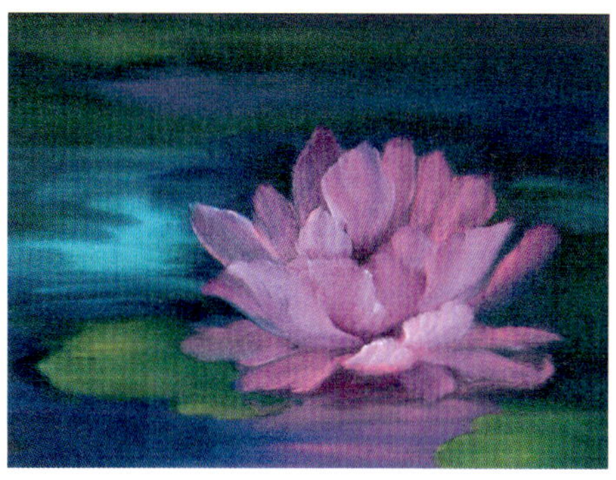

11. Working forward, highlight the front petals.

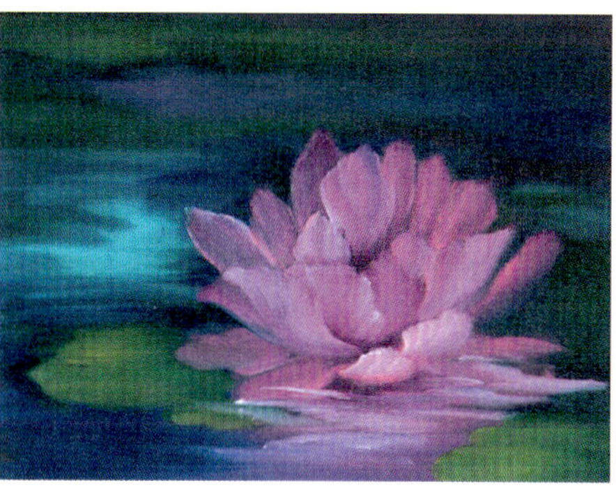

12. With mixtures of White, Magenta and Turquoise on the 3/4" brush, 'swirl' in water at the base of the flower.

13. Add stamens with the small round brush and thinned Yellow. Highlight the leaves with Yellow, using the 3/4" brush. Then, use the small round brush to add the water drops and the liner brush with thinned color of your choice to sign your water posie.

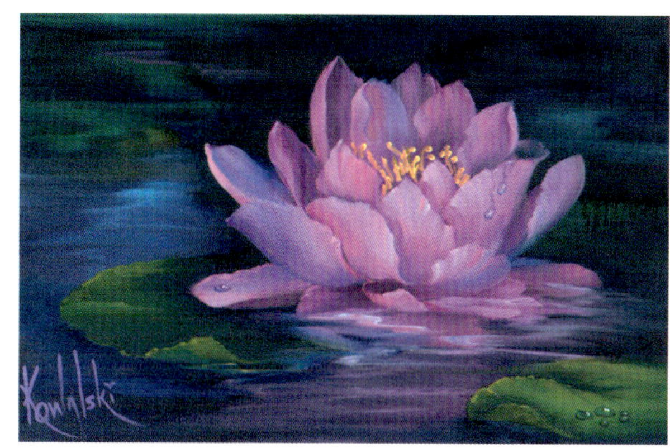

Painting Water Drops

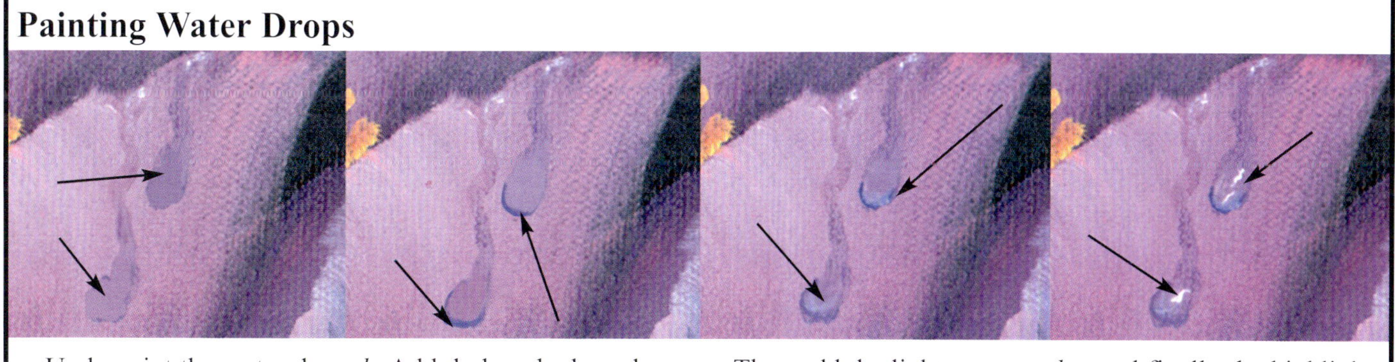

a. Underpaint the water drop with the small round brush and a dark mixture.

b. Add darker shadowed area.

c. Then add the light area...

d. ...and finally the highlight.

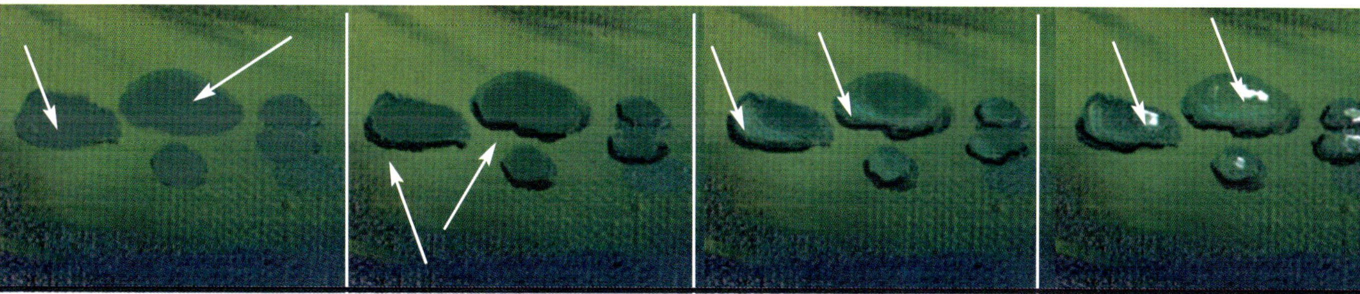

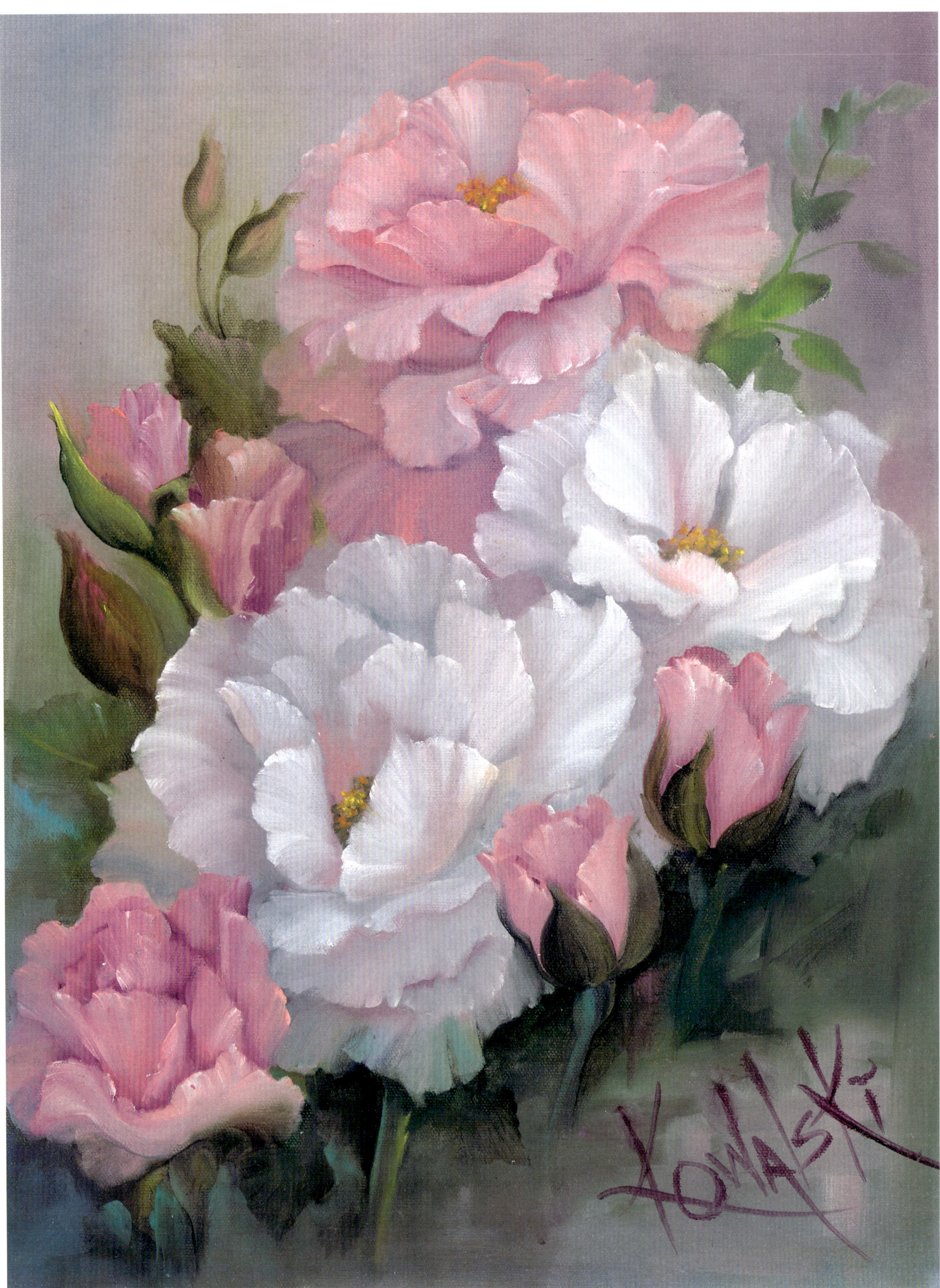
Kowalski

10. Guadalupe Roses

In 1541, Mexico was on the verge of an uprising due to the ill treatment of people by Spanish soldiers. The bishop had prayed for peace, asking for roses as a sign that his prayers would be heard. Castilian roses (Our Lady of Guadalupe roses) appeared miraculously in the midst of winter snow.

Materials:

Bob Ross Soft Oil Colors:
Alizarin Crimson
Black
Cadmium Yellow Light
Cadmium Orange
Dusty Rose
Mauve
Sap Green
Titanium White
Turquoise
Ultramarine Blue

Bob Ross Mediums:
Bob Ross Oil Paint Medium
Bob Ross Odorless Thinner
Liquid Opal

Bob Ross Brushes:
1" Landscape Brush
3/4" Floral Brush
1/2" Floral Brush
Floral Filbert Brush
Small Round Floral Brush
#2 Liner Brush

Other Materials:
Bob Ross Disposable Floral Palette
1 Canvas (18x24)

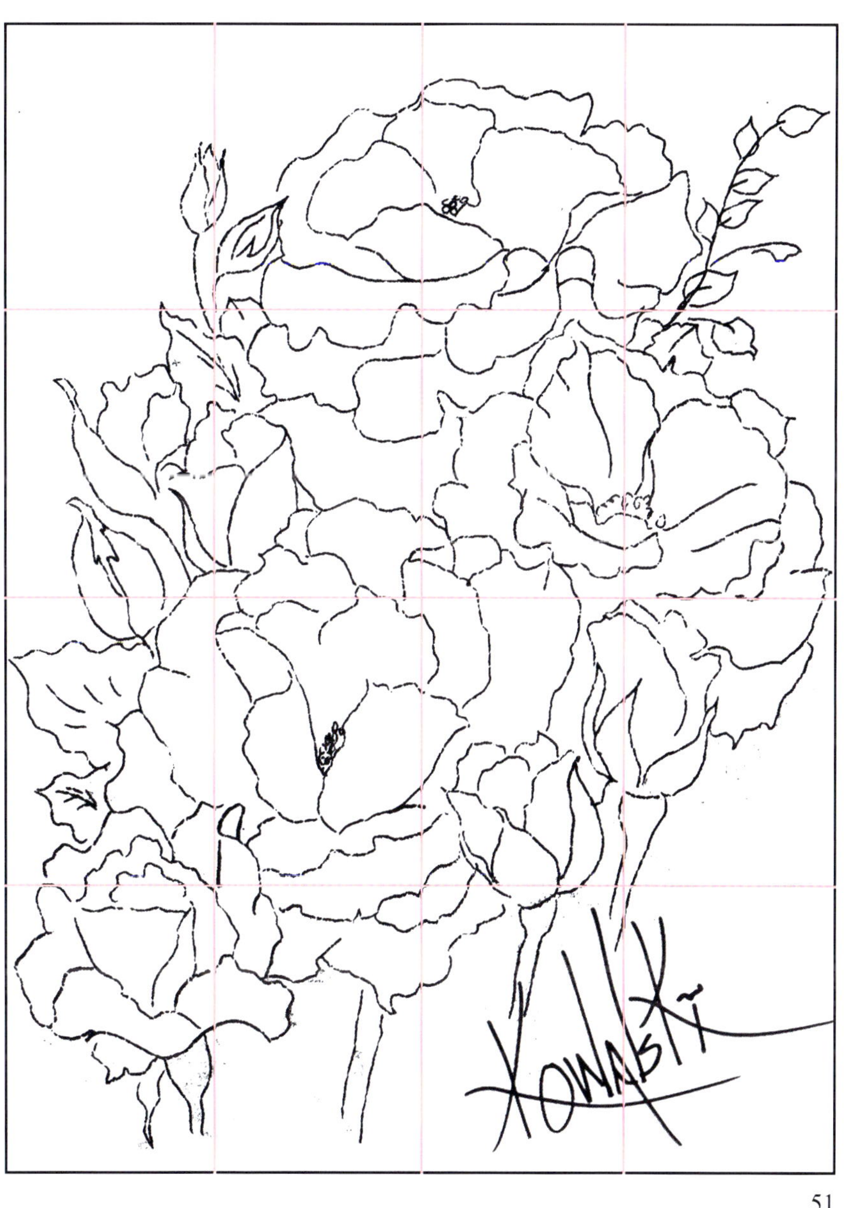

10. Guadalupe Roses

Progressional Steps

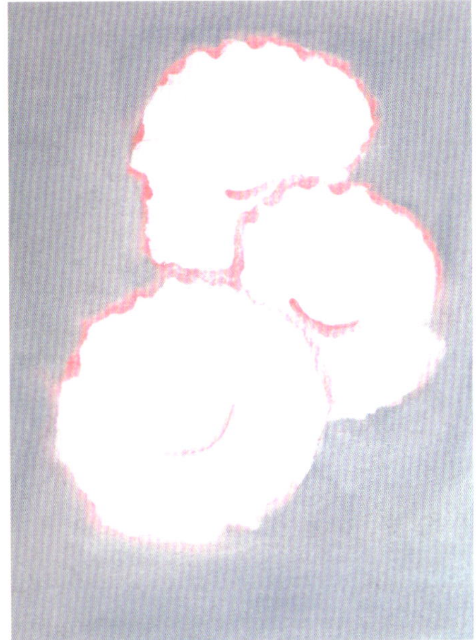

1. Lightly sketch the flower placement with thinned Dusty Rose and the small round brush. Carefully avoiding the flowers, use the 1" brush and criss-cross strokes to add Liquid Opal to the background.

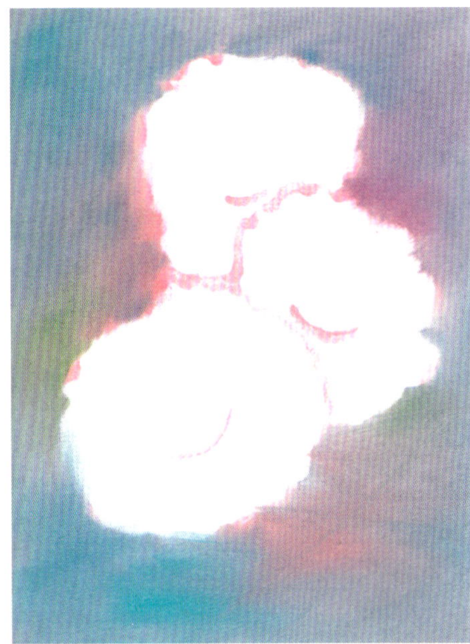

2. Continue using the 1" brush and loose criss-cross strokes to add various mixtures of Mauve, Pink, Turquoise and Green. Lightly blend the entire background.

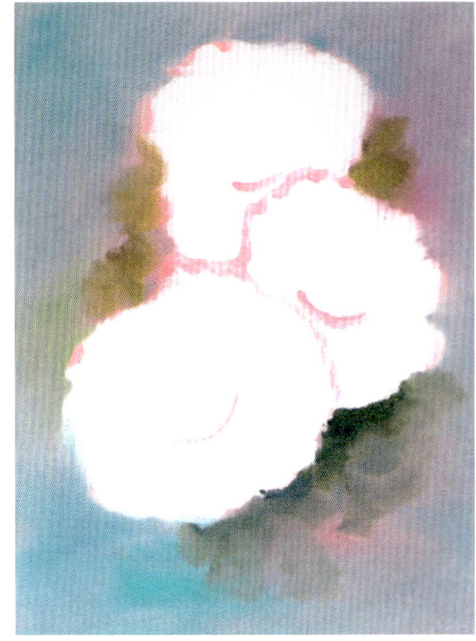

3. Add the dark foliage areas with criss-cross strokes and the 3/4" brush. Use mixtures of Green, Blue and Crimson.

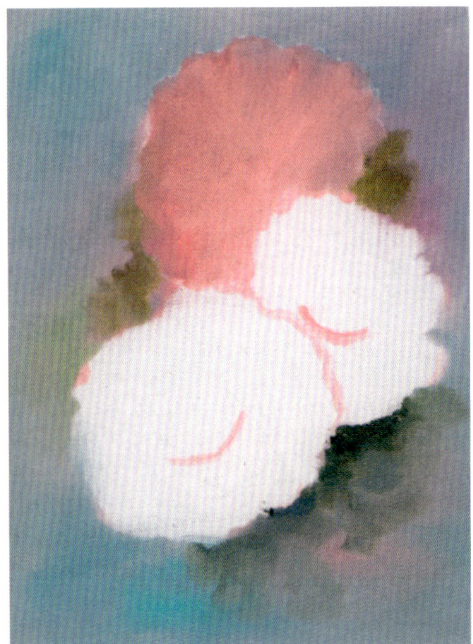

4. With the 1/2" brush, underpaint the Pink rose with Dusty Rose which has been thinned with Oil Paint Medium.

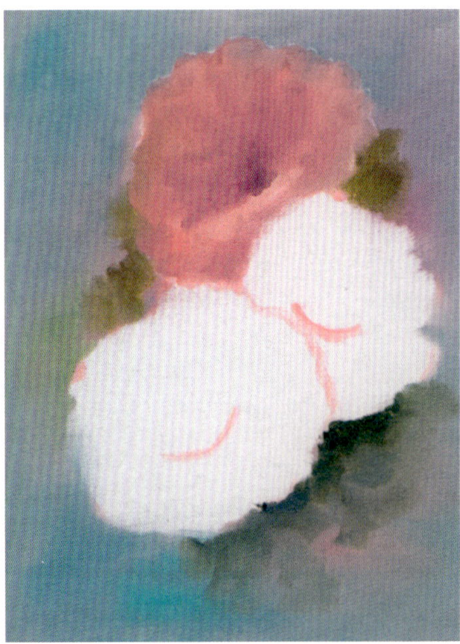

5. Add Mauve to the center of the flower and blend outward, in the direction the rose is facing

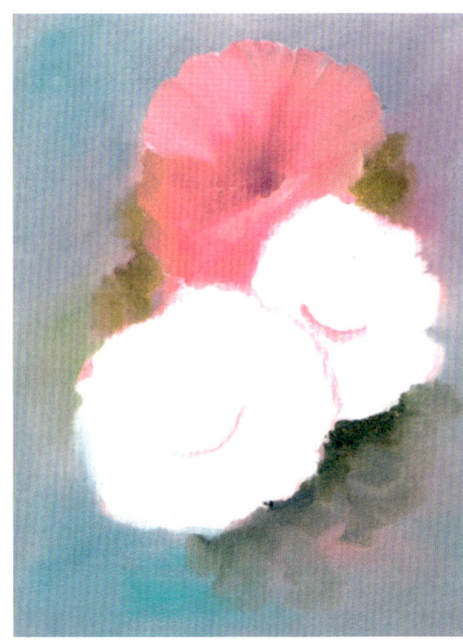

6. Highlight the rose, one petal at a time with White which has been tinted with a small amount of Dusty Rose. Starting at the out-side edge of each petal, direct overlapping strokes towards the center of the rose.

10. Guadalupe Roses

Progressional Steps

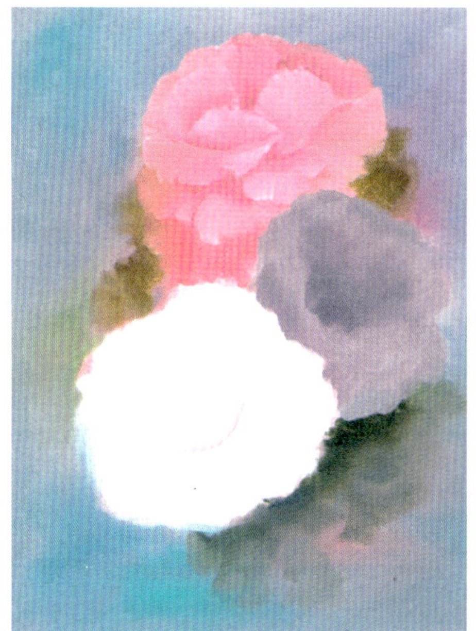

7. When the Pink rose is complete, underpaint the White rose with a thinned mixture of White, Black, Mauve and Dusty Rose. Use less White for the center.

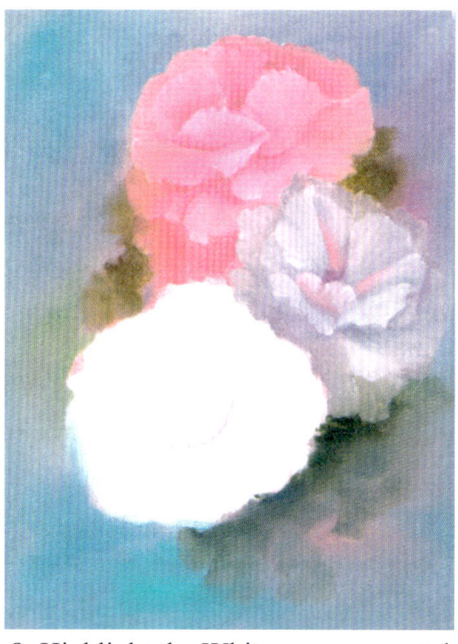

8. Highlight the White rose, one petal at a time with White.

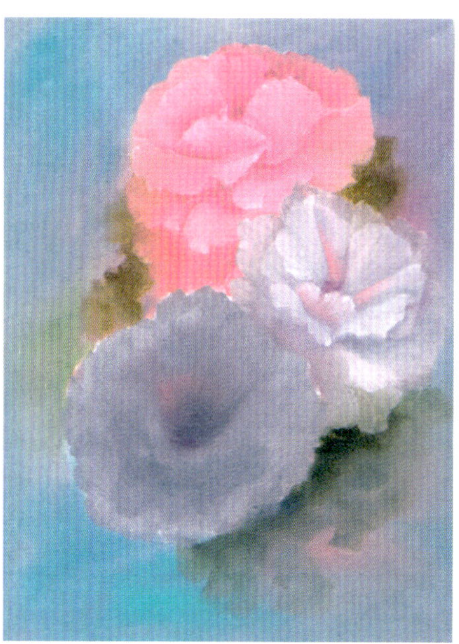

9. Underpaint the third rose again with a thin mixture of White, Black, Mauve and Dusty Rose. Use less White for the center.

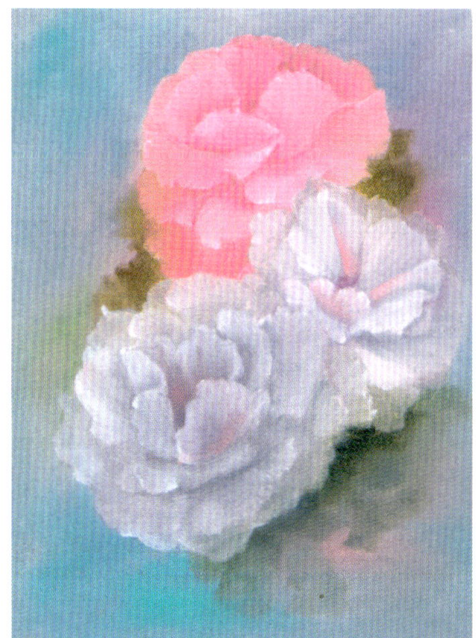

10. Highlight the final rose, one petal at a time with White.

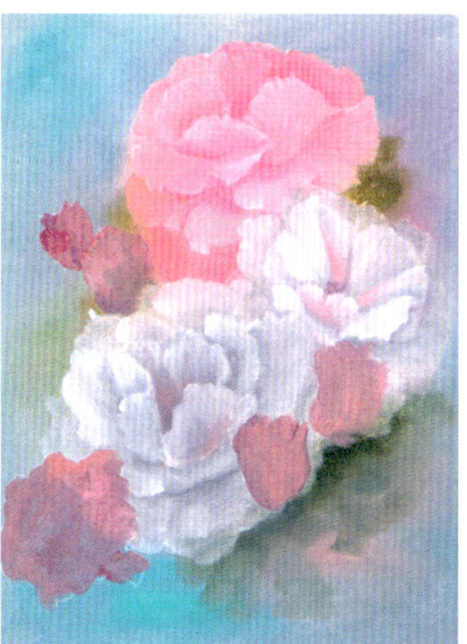

11. Underpaint the buds with a thin mixture of Rose and Mauve. Suggest the petals with White. Add the calyx-es with Blue, Green and Yellow.

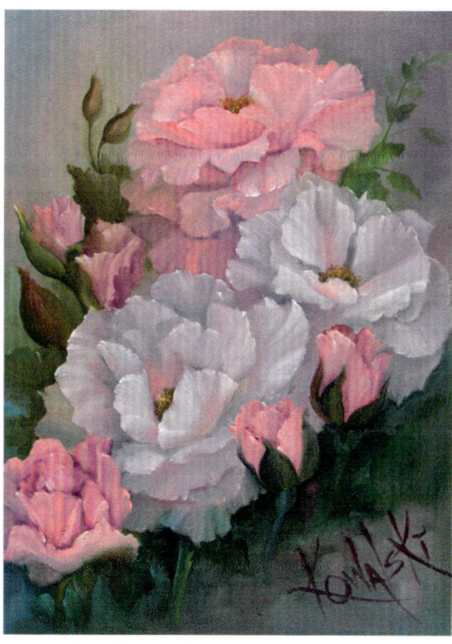

12. Use dots of Mauve, Green and Yellow to add the centers of the roses. With Blue and Green add final leaves and buds. Ole!

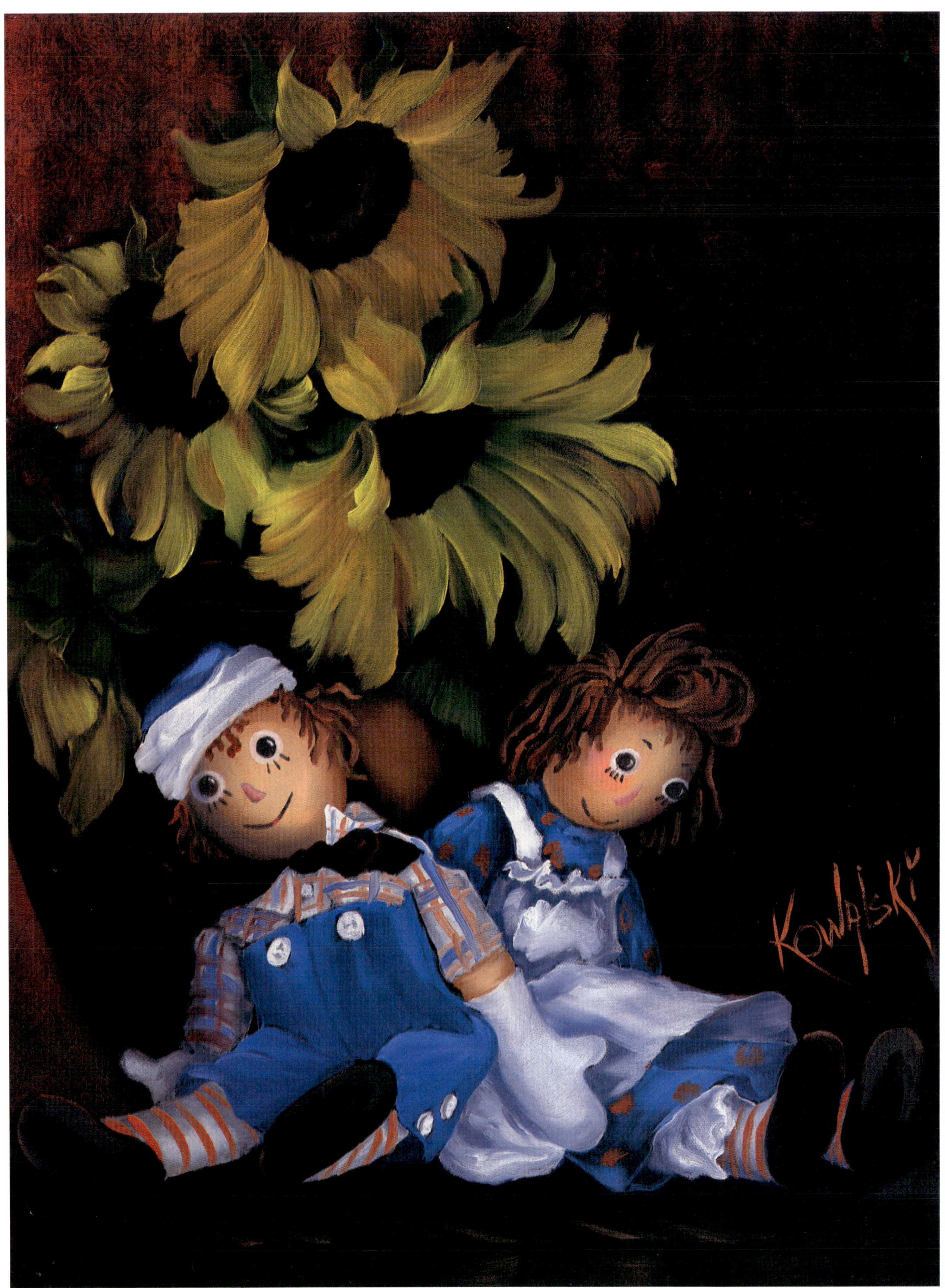
KOWALSKI

11. Best Friends

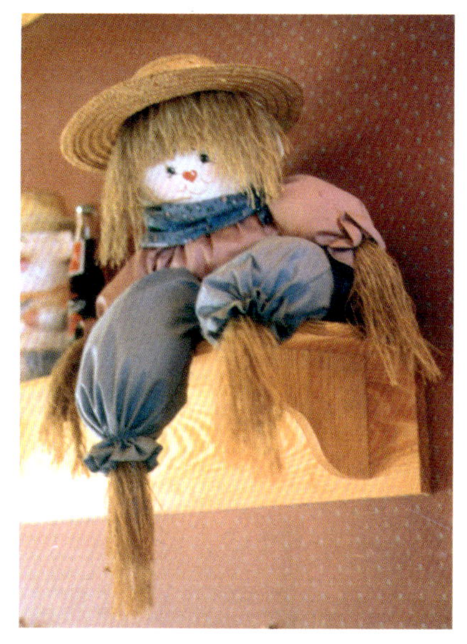

Raggedy Ann was created by Johnny Gruelle in 1915. Her brother, Raggedy Andy, was introduced in 1920. Rag dolls and flowers make perfect painting partners; all created using long, flowing brushstrokes of vibrant colors. Try painting other dolls with other flowers. They're sure to please a young person in your life.

Materials Needed:

Bob Ross Soft Oil Colors:
Alizarin Crimson
Cadmium Orange
Cadmium Red Medium
Cadmium Yellow
Ivory Black
Sap Green
Titanium White
Turquoise
Ultramarine Blue

Bob Ross Mediums:
Black Gesso
Oil Paint Medium
Bob Ross Odorless Thinner

Bob Ross Brushes:
1" Landscape Brush
1/2" Floral Brush
3/4" Floral Brush
Small Round Floral Brush
#2 Liner Brush

Other Materials:
Bob Ross Disposable Floral Palette
Canvas (18x24)
Foam Applicator
Dressmakers Tracing Paper, *optional*
Plastic Wrap

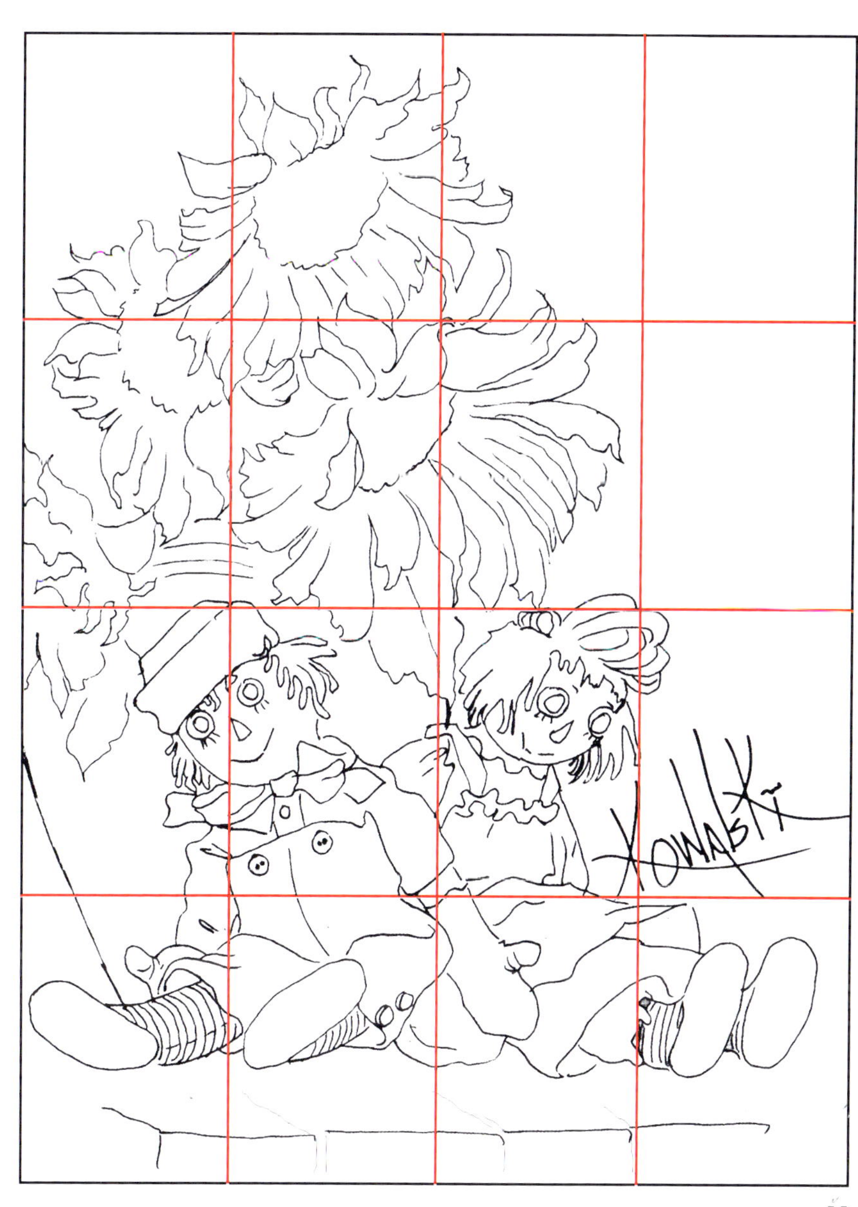

11. Best Friends

Progressional Steps

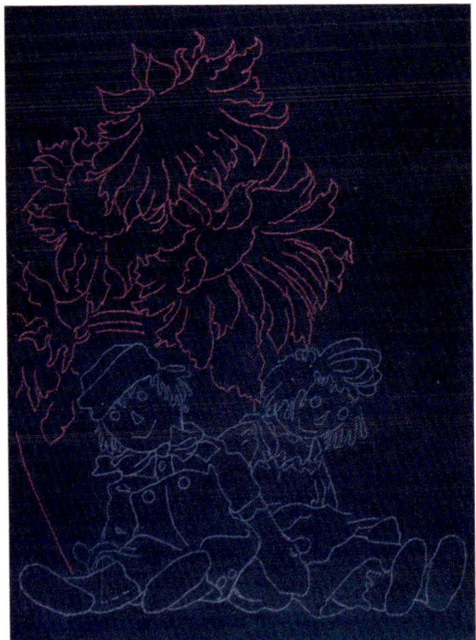

1. Use the foam applicator to cover the canvas with Black Gesso and allow to dry completely. Sketch the dolls and flowers with thinned color and the small round brush or transfer the pattern with Dressmaker's Tracing Paper.

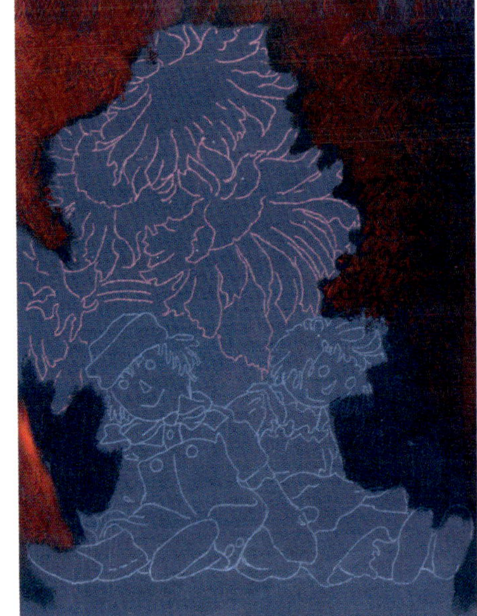

2. Use the 3/4" brush to cover the background with a very small amount of Oil Paint Medium. Working from light to dark, start at the top, left side of the background and add a small amount of Cadmium Red Medium.

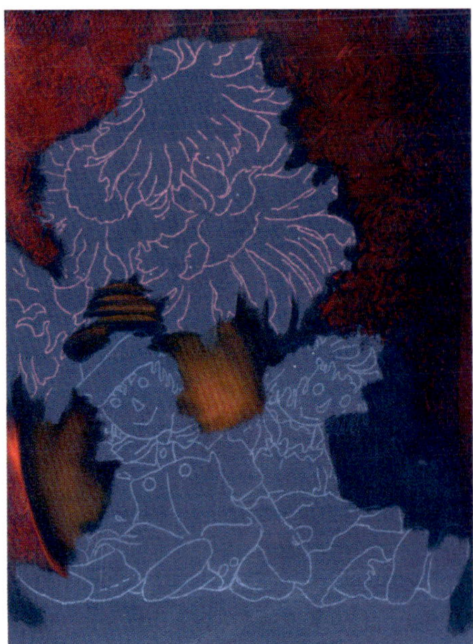

3. Use crumpled plastic wrap to 'mottle' the background color. With equal parts of Green and Crimson, paint the clay flower pot with the 1/2" brush. Add Orange to the light, right side of the pot and Blue to the dark, left side.

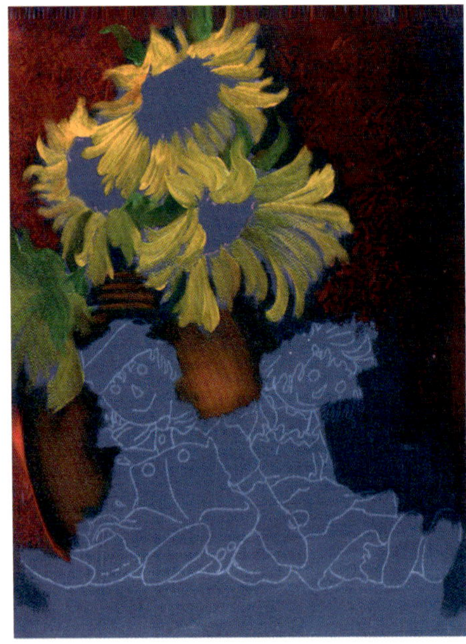

4. Use the 1/2" brush to underpaint the sunflowers with mixtures of Yellow, Orange, Sap Green and Alizarin Crimson. Use just enough Oil Paint Medium to ensure a flowing consistency.

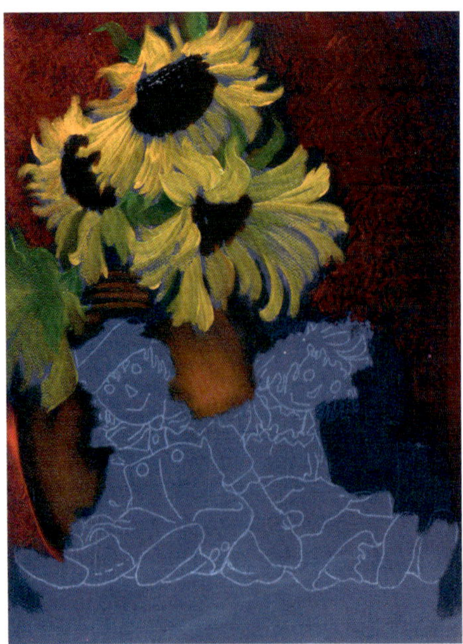

5. Add the sunflower centers with the 1/2" brush and your Brown mixture made from equal parts of Alizarin Crimson and Sap Green.

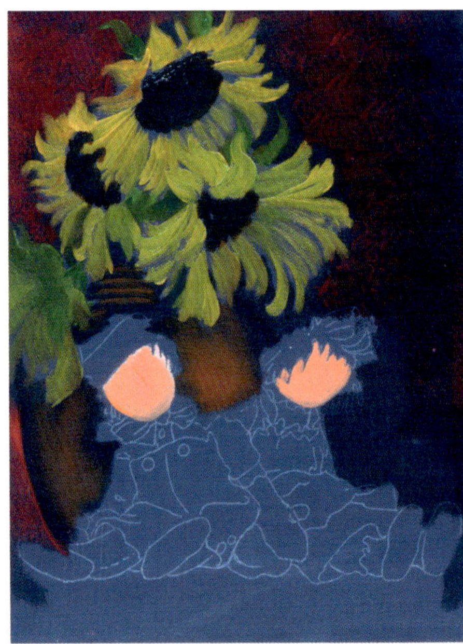

6. Paint the faces of the dolls with the 1/2" brush and equal parts of Titanium White and Cadmium Orange.

11. Best Friends

Progressional Steps

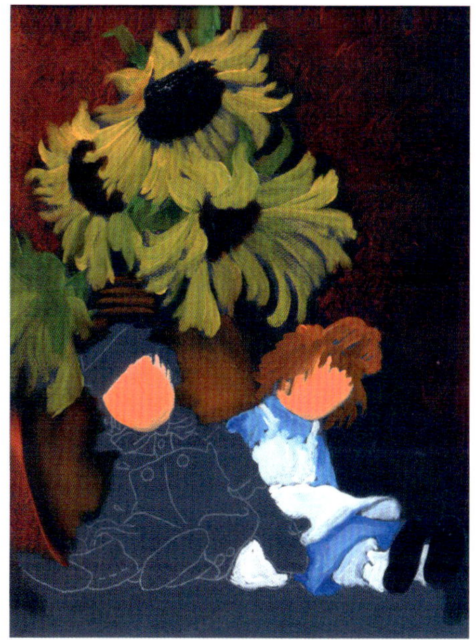

7. The blue clothes are painted with a mixture of Ultramarine Blue and Turquoise. Paint the shoes with Black.

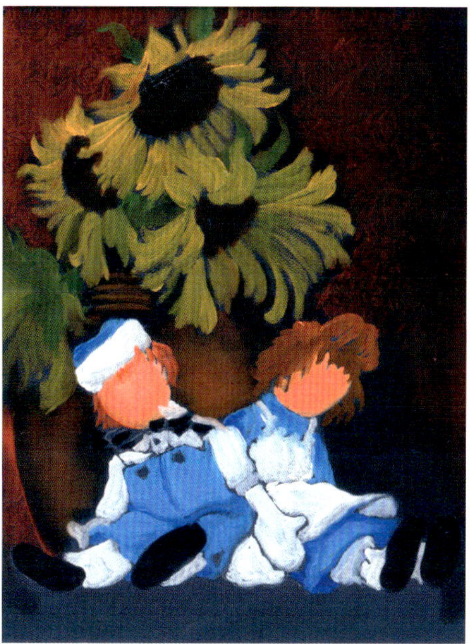

8. The white clothing on both dolls is White which has been tinted with Yellow and Orange. Add Blue to the mixture for the shadowed areas. Use the 1/2" brush and the small round brush as necessary.

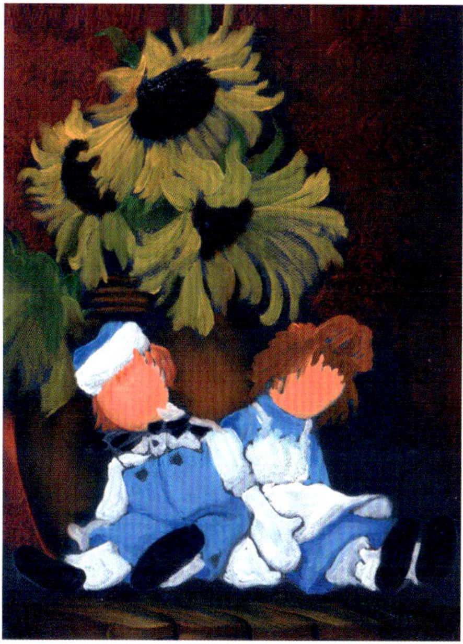

9. Load the 3/4" brush with your brown mixture which has been thinned with Oil Paint Medium to indicate the wooden table top. Highlight with mixtures of Orange and Yellow.

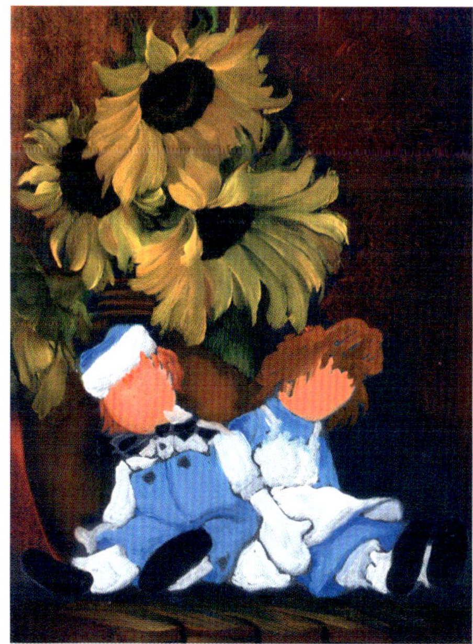

10. With Green and Blue, add the sunflower calyxes and the suggestion of a leaf behind Raggedy Ann. Highlight the sunflowers with various mixtures of Yellow and White.

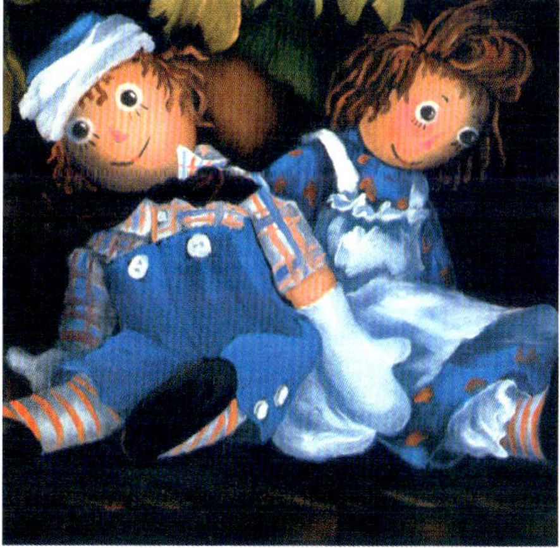

11. Shadow the doll's faces with Blue. Use a small amount of Alizarin Crimson to make Ann's rosy cheeks.Then use the small round brush to add final details: Red and Blue for Andy's shirt, Red flowers on Ann's dress, Black and White eyes, Alizarin Crimson with White for the nose and mouth.

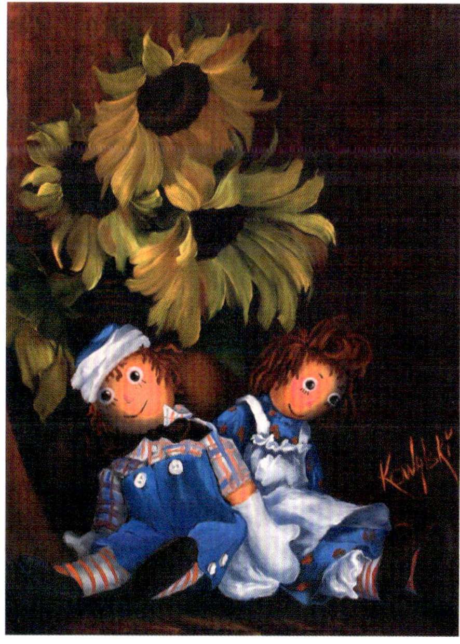

12. The dolls' hair is Brown and Orange. Buttons are White and stripes on socks are added with Red. Finally, sign your name with pride and enjoy your new friends!

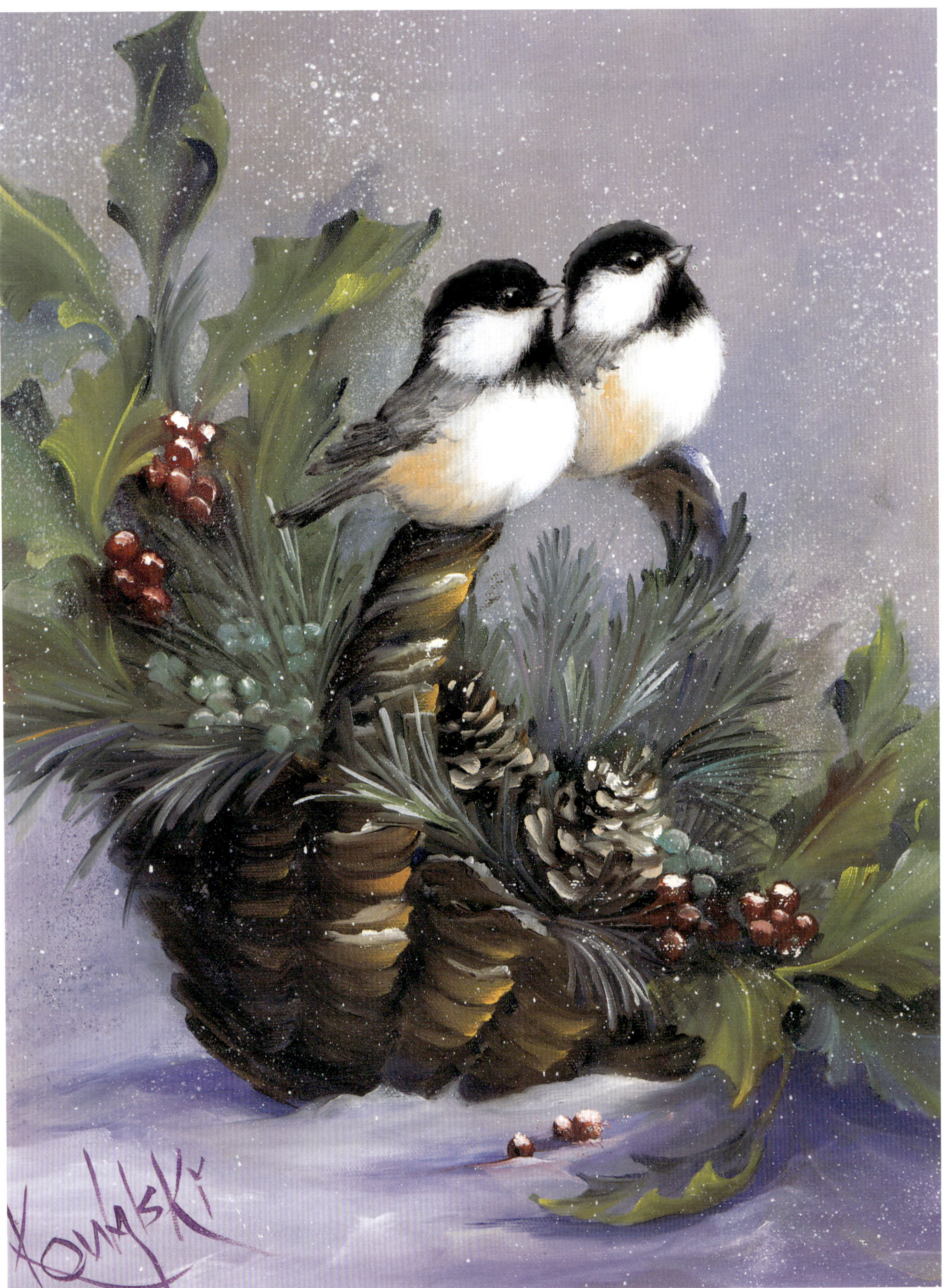
Kowalski

12. Chickadees

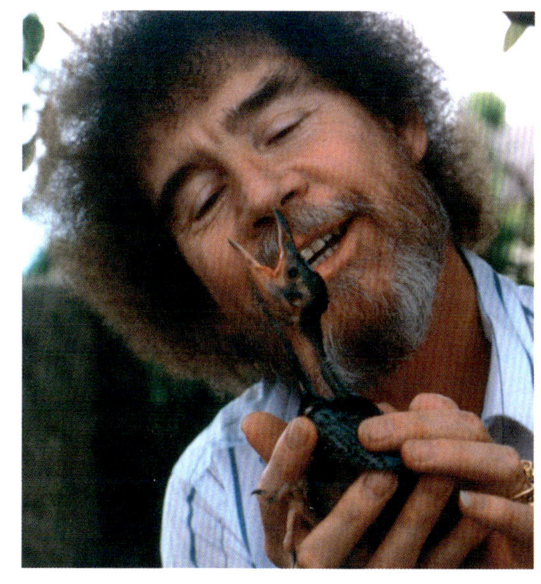

Who can enjoy these two, tiny winter visitors and not think of Bob?

Painting Tip
Enlarge the basket of foliage for an 18x24 canvas, but do not paint your Chickadees larger than actual size, or you'll have Eagle-dees!

Ellen Tye,CRWI

Materials:

Bob Ross Soft Oil Colors:
Alizarin Crimson
Black
Cadmium Yellow Light
Cadmium Orange
Cadmium Red Light
Mauve
Sap Green
Titanium White
Turquoise
Ultramarine Blue

Bob Ross Mediums:
Bob Ross Oil Paint Medium
Bob Ross Odorless Thinner
Bob Ross Gray Gesso

Bob Ross Brushes:
1" Landscape Brush
3/4" Floral Brush
1/2" Floral Brush
Floral Filbert Brush
Small Round Floral Brush
Floral Fan Brush
#2 Liner Brush

Other Materials:
Foam Applicator
Dressmakers Tracing Paper
Black Permanent Felt-Tipped Marker
12x16 Canvas

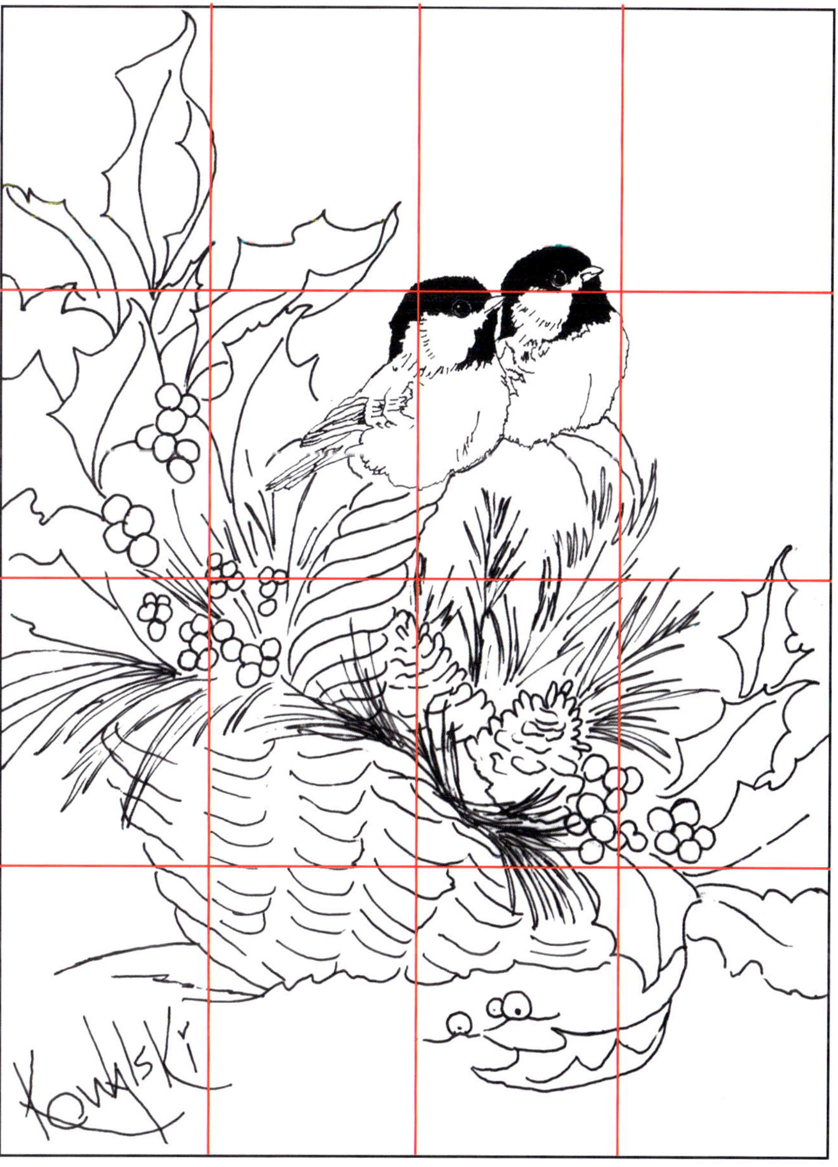

12. Chickadees

Progressional Steps

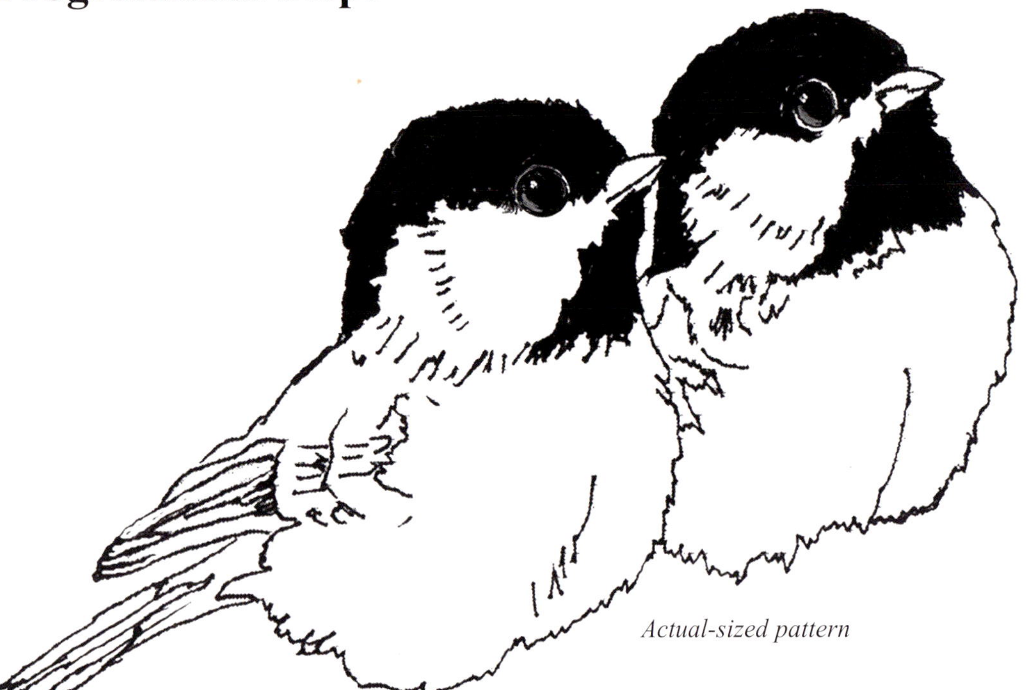

Actual-sized pattern

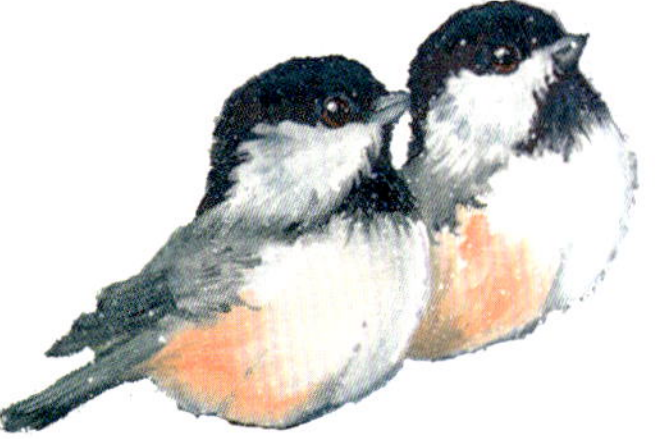

2. 'Overpaint' the chickadees with the small round brush, and mixtures of Oil Paint Medium, Ivory Black and Titanium White. Add a small amount of Cadmium Orange to the tummy and a dot of White to the eye.

1. Canvas Preparation
Begin by using the foam applicator to cover your entire canvas with a thin, even coat of Gray Gesso. When the canvas is dry, use Dressmakers Tracing Paper to transfer the basket placement and the chickadees to your canvas. Then, 'underpaint' the black-areas of the birds with a permanent, black, felt-tipped marker: tops of their heads, throats and eyes. (Or, you may prefer to use a synthetic brush and Bob Ross Liquid Black Acrylic.)

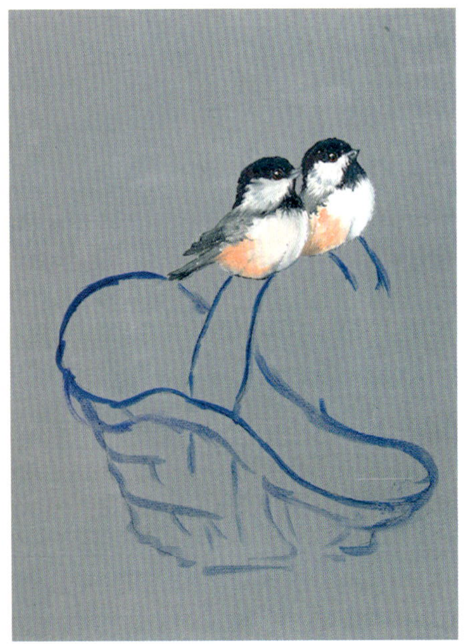

3. Use thinned Blue to loosely sketch the basket. Add the background with the 1" brush and various mixtures of Oil Paint Medium, Blue, Mauve and White.

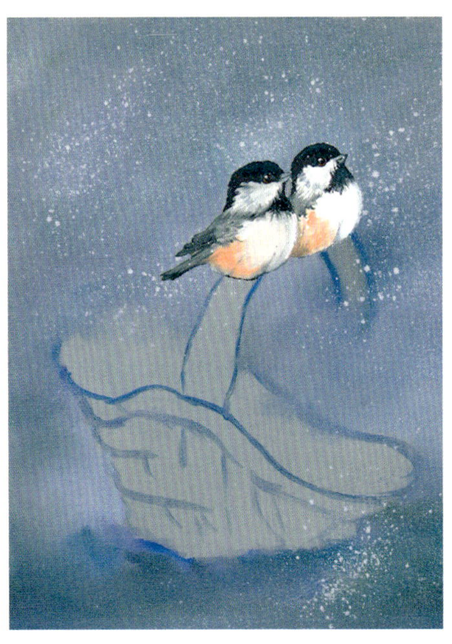

4. With a very, very thin mixture of Paint Thinner and Titanium White on the fan brush, spray the background to create the snowy effect.

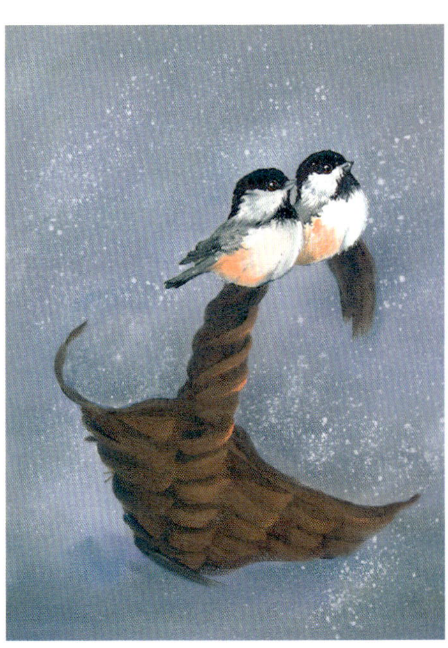

5. Paint the basket with the filbert brush and a Brown mixture made from equal parts of Alizarin Crimson and Sap Green. *Refer to the Basic How-To Photos.*

Progressional Steps

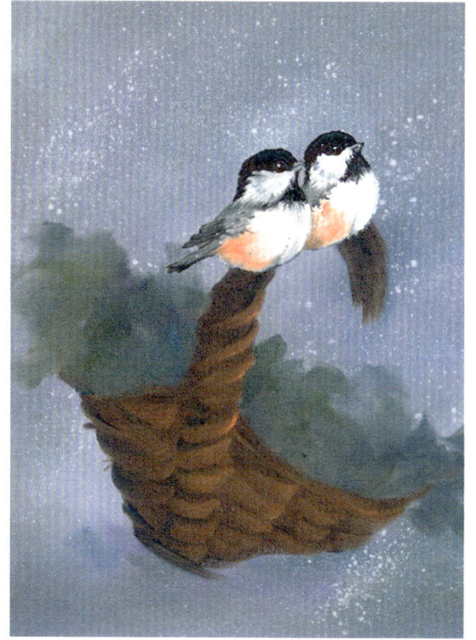

6. Loosely block in foliage with Blue and Green.

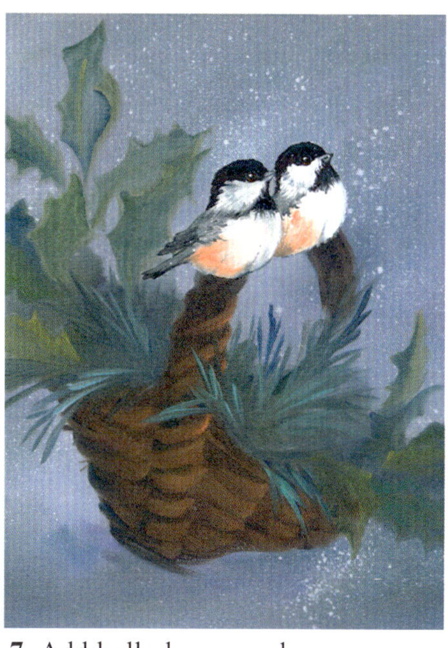

7. Add holly leaves and evergreens with Blue and Green.

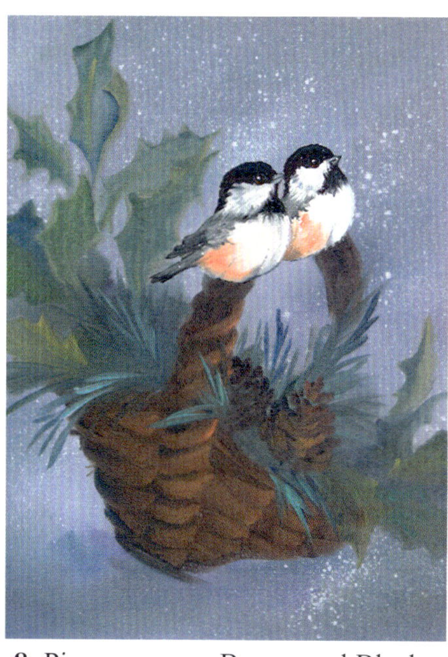

8. Pine cones are Brown and Black. Berries are Red, others Turquoise.

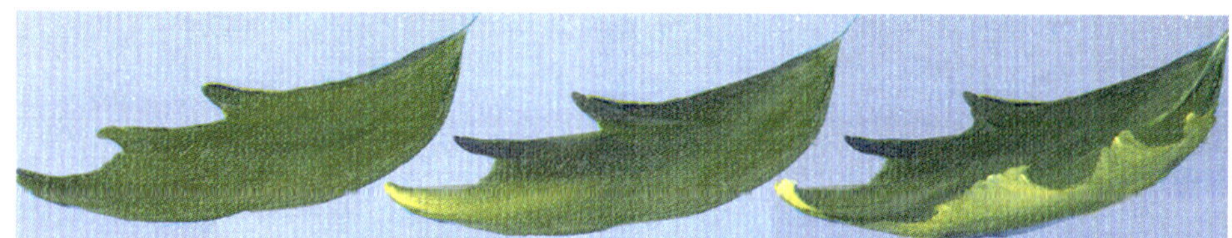

Painting holly leaves.

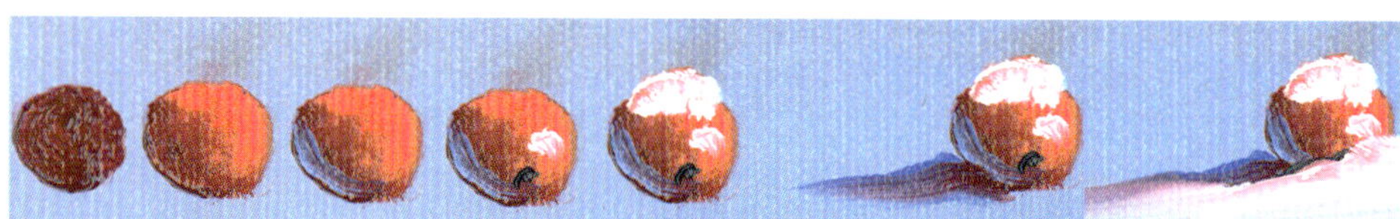

Painting snow-capped berries.

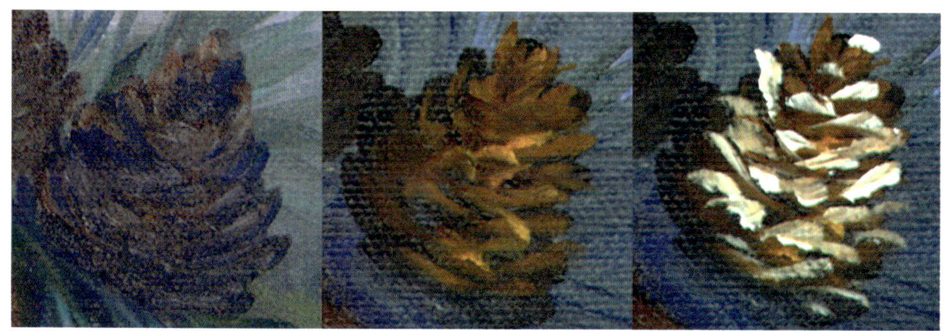

Painting pine cones.

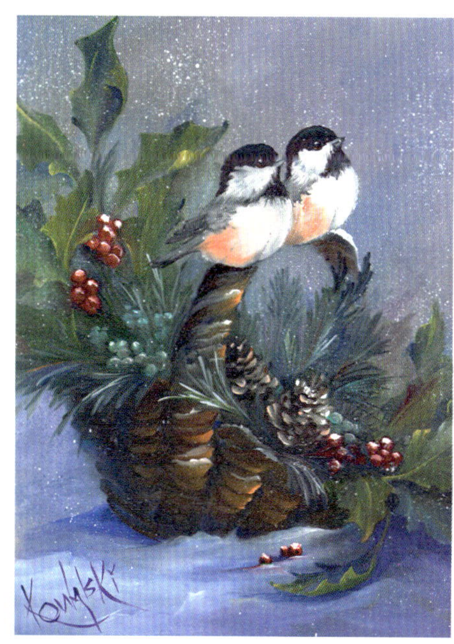

9. Highlight leaves and evergreens with mixtures of Yellow, Red Light, Turquoise and Mauve. Use White to add snow to the basket, evergreens, berries, pine cones and the base of the basket. Additional leaves and berries complete your painting.

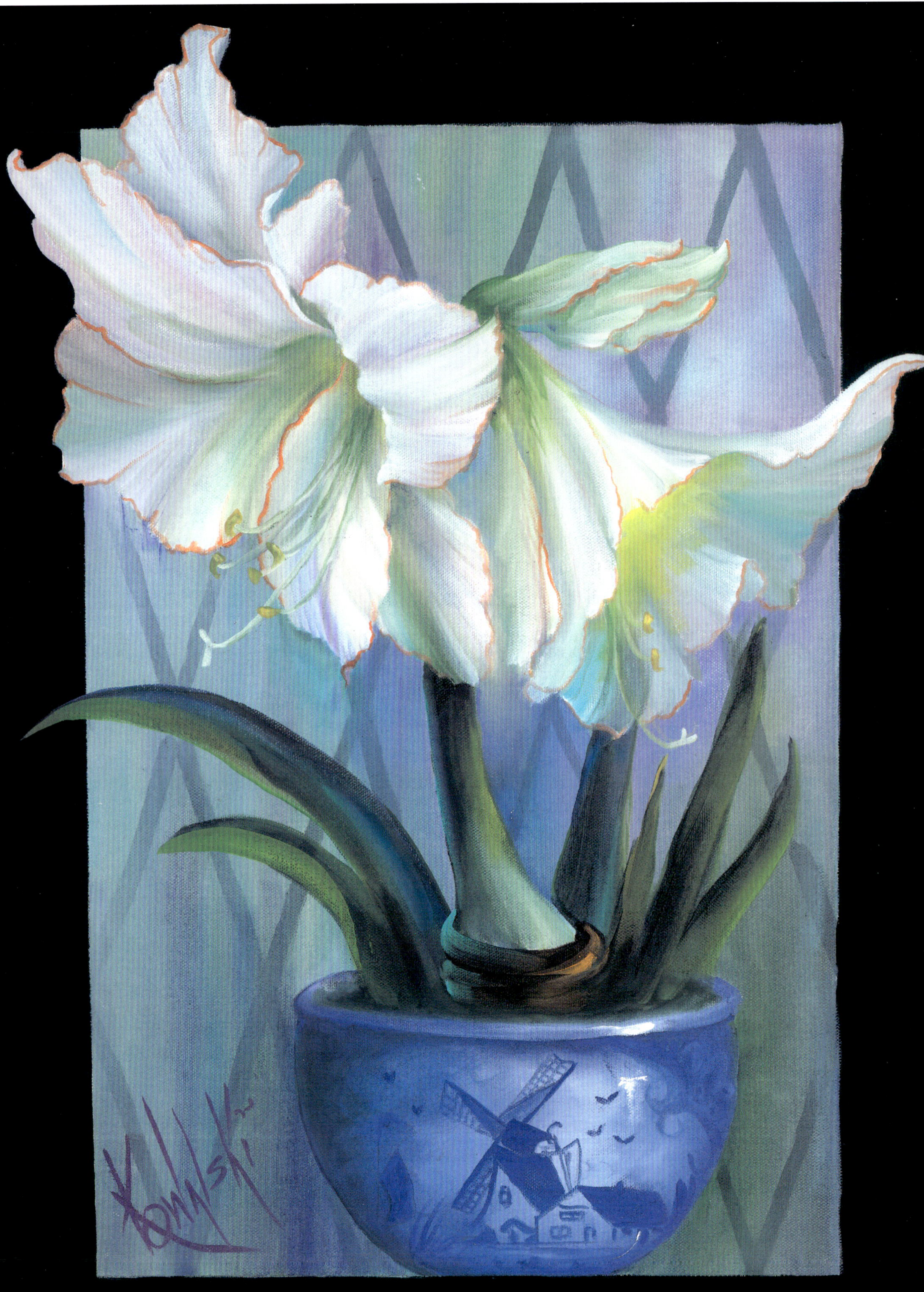

13. Bob Ross Amaryllis

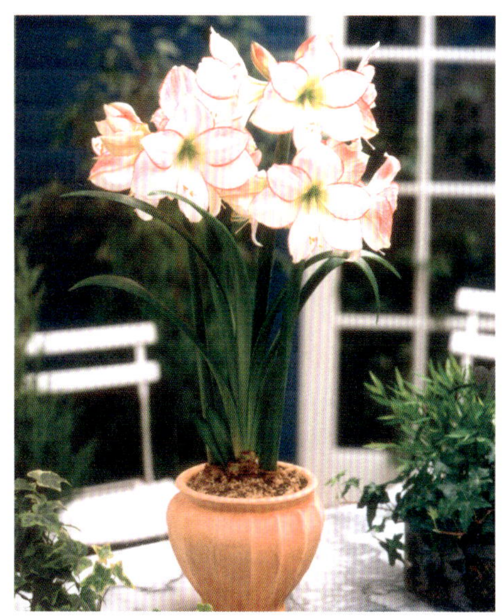

This beautiful white amaryllis whose petal edges have been 'signed in red by Bob' was officially named "The Bob Ross Memorial Amaryllis" by Leo Berpee & Sons of the Netherlands in 1997.

Materials:

Bob Ross Soft Oil Colors:

Alizarin Crimson
Cadmium Yellow Light
Cadmium Orange
Cadmium Red Light
Cadmium Red Medium
Mauve
Sap Green
Titanium White
Turquoise
Ultramarine Blue

Bob Ross Mediums:

Bob Ross Oil Paint Medium
Bob Ross Odorless Thinner
Black Gesso

Bob Ross Brushes:

1" Landscape Brush
3/4" Floral Brush
1/2" Floral Brush
Floral Filbert Brush
Small Round Floral Brush
Floral Fan Brush
#2 Liner Brush

Other Materials:

Bob Ross Disposable Floral Palette
1 Canvas (18x24)
Foam Applicator
Masking Tape

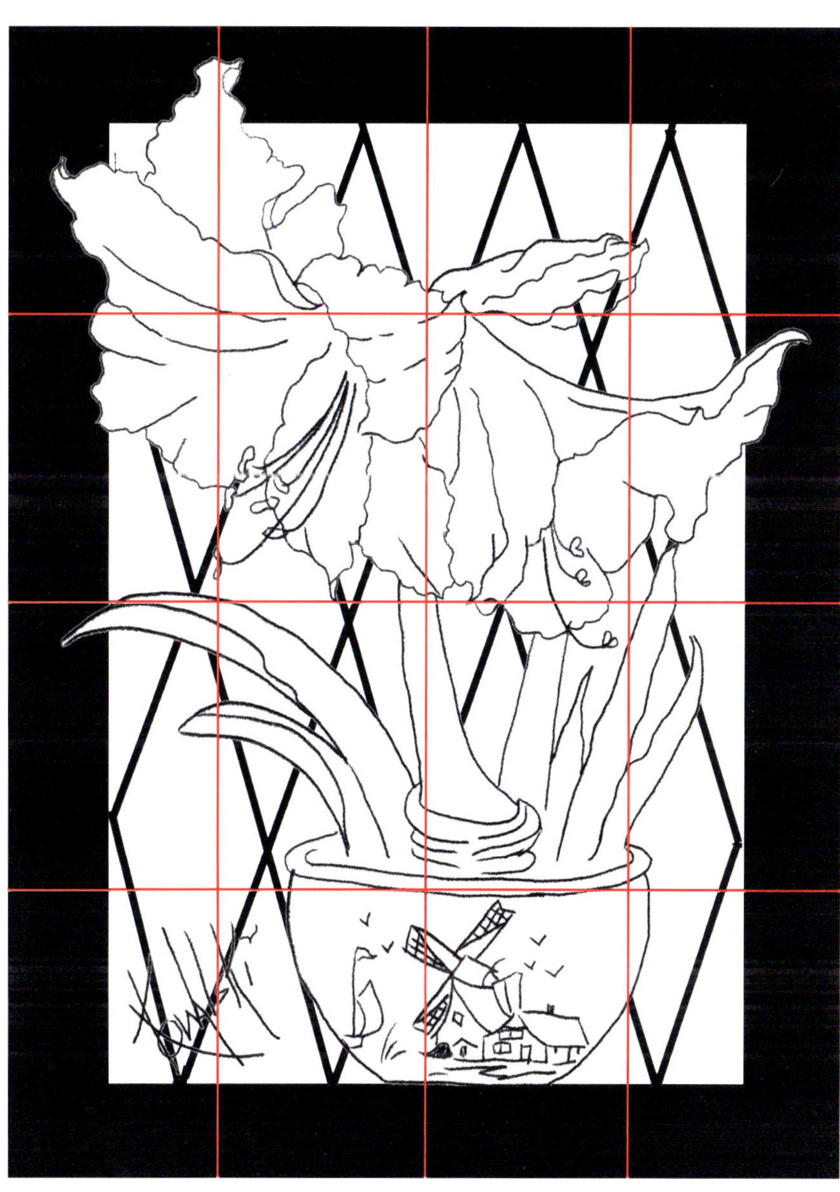

13. Bob Ross Dutch Amaryllis

Progressional Steps

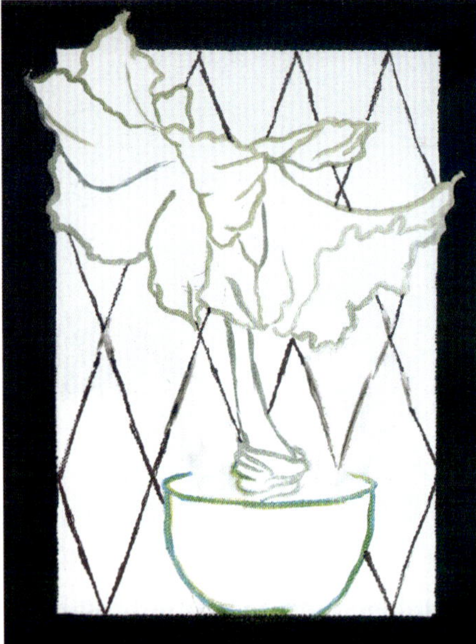

1. Start by using the foam applicator and Black Gesso to add a two-inch border and 'window panes' to the canvas. Allow to dry completely. Use the small round brush with thinned Green to lightly sketch the placement of the Amaryllis and Delft pot.

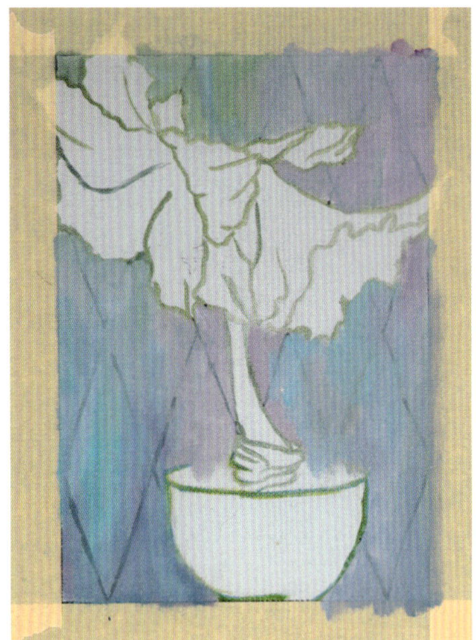

2. Protect the border with masking tape. With the 1" brush, add the background with mixtures of Blue, Green, Turquoise, Mauve and White thinned with Oil Paint Medium. When the background is complete, remove the protective masking tape.

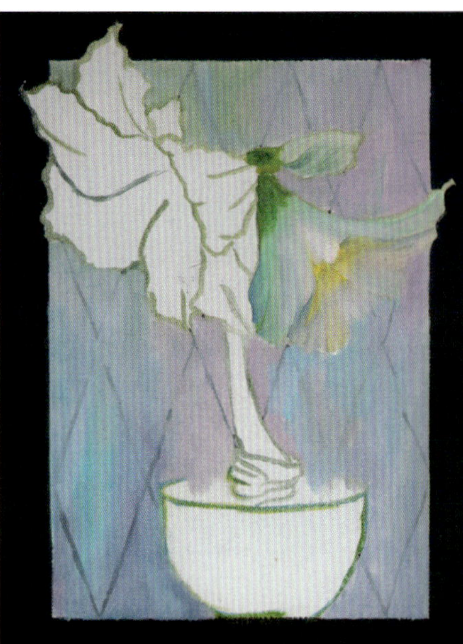

3. Underpaint the buds with White which has been tinted with various mixtures of Blue, Green and Turquoise. Add Yellow to the center of the half-open flower. Use long, flowing, overlapping strokes directed towards the base of the buds.

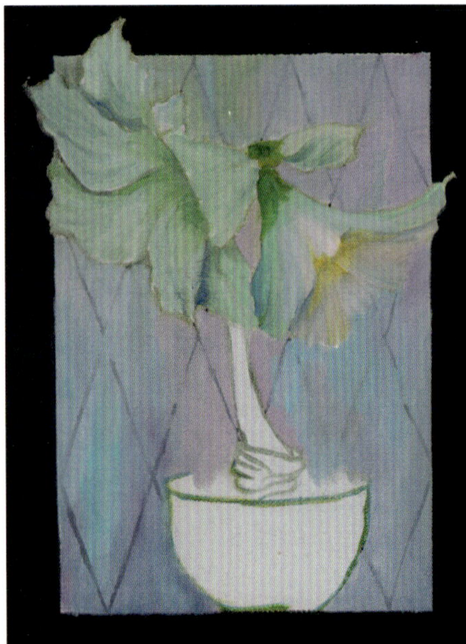

4. Continue using the 3/4" brush to loosely underpaint the Amaryllis, one petal at a time, again with White which has been tinted with various mixtures of Blue, Green and Turquoise.

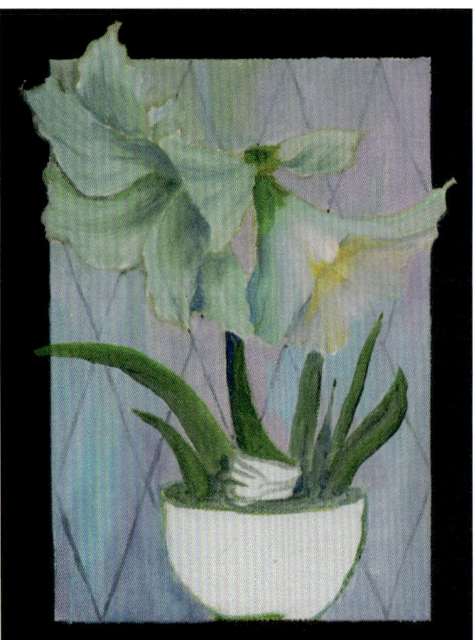

5. Use long, flowing, overlapping strokes all directed towards the center of the flower. Add the dark shadowed areas of the flower with Blue and Green. Then, with the 3/4" brush, add the fat stem and tapered leaves with mixtures of Blue, Green and Yellow.

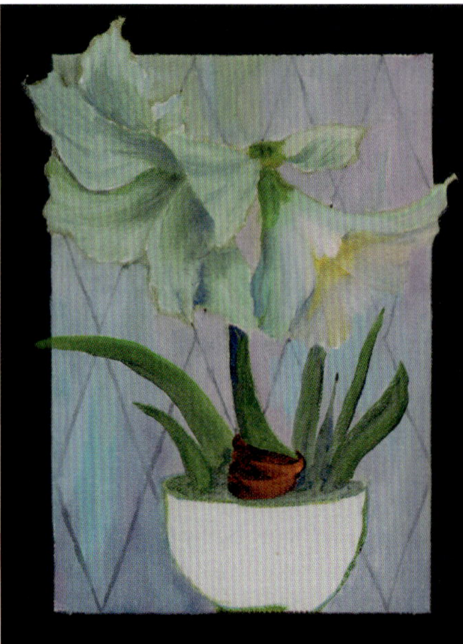

6. Add the base of the stem (the amaryllis bulb) with Brown made from equal parts of Alizarin Crimson and Sap Green. Highlight the base with Orange.

Progressional Steps

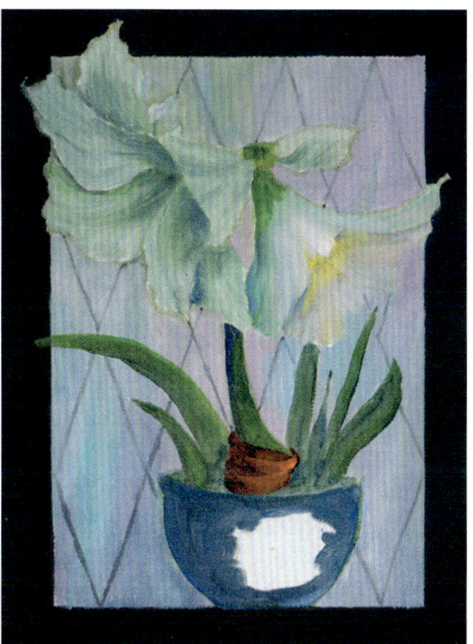

7. With the 1/2" brush and loose criss-cross strokes, paint the dark area of the Delft pot with a mixture of Blue, Green, Turquoise and Mauve to which you have added a small amount of White.

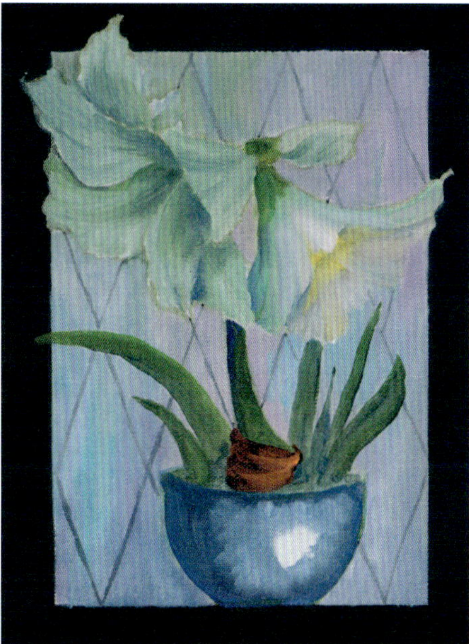

8. Add additional White to the mixture and again use criss-cross strokes to paint the middle value of the pot.

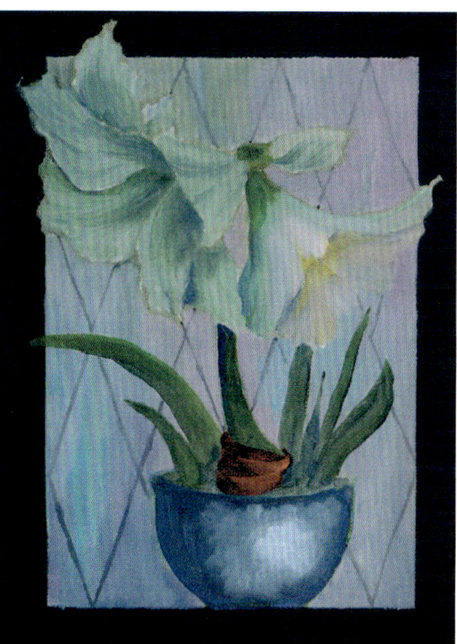

9. Add the lightest area of the pot with White which has been tinted with a very, very small amount of Yellow. Again, use loose criss-cross strokes.

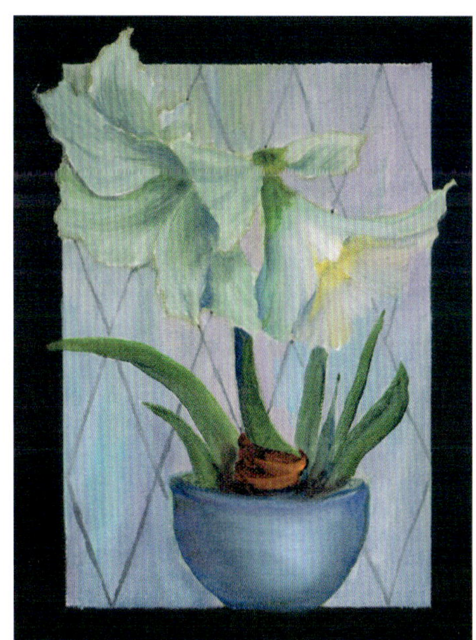

10. With a clean, dry brush, and very little pressure, lightly merge the three values with criss-cross strokes. Then, blend with the fan brush and sweeping, horizontal strokes.

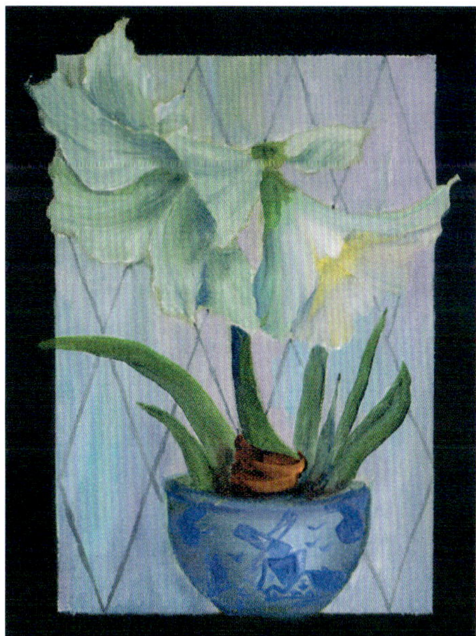

11. Add the Delft pattern to the pot with the small round brush and Ultramarine Blue. Final highlights on the pot are pure White. Add stamens with the filbert brush and Green and Yellow. Stamen tips are Orange.

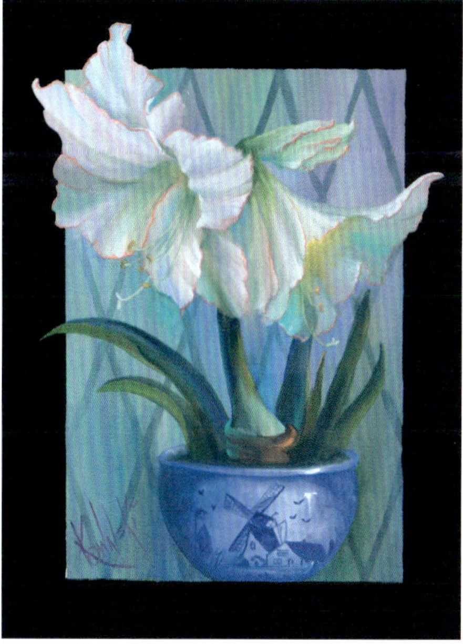

12. Highlight the leaves with Yellow and the base of the stem with White. Use the liner brush with thinned Reds to 'edge' the petals and to sign your masterpiece.

General Information

This section of the book is devoted to information that is not contained elsewhere in the text. If you have any questions which have not been answered, please feel free to write to us c/o The Bob Ross Company. Please include a stamped, self-addressed envelope with your letter and we will try our best to answer any of your questions.

CAN I USE ANY TYPE OF ART PRODUCTS FOR THIS METHOD OF PAINTING?

All of the paintings in this book were produced with products specially designed for this method of painting. To achieve the best results from your efforts, I strongly recommend that you use the only products designed specifically for this technique. Always insist that the supplies you purchased have the "Bob Ross" label. This will assure that you are receiving the finest and most suitable products available.

WHERE CAN I OBTAIN MATERIALS SPECIFICALLY DESIGNED FOR THIS TECHNIQUE OF PAINTING FLOWERS?

The unique products used throughout this book are available at art stores throughout the United States, Canada and numerous other foreign countries. They may be purchased individually or in kit form. All of the products may be ordered by mail or via toll-free telephone, and delivered directly to your door from the following address:

The Bob Ross Company
P.O. Box 946
Sterling, Virginia 20167-0946
Tel: 1-800-BOB-ROSS (1-800-262-7677)
www.bobross.com

All orders to the Bob Ross Company are shipped promptly. Dealer inquiries are always welcome.

ARE CLASSES AVAILABLE FOR THIS METHOD?

There is a select group of highly-qualified instructors who are not only accredited to teach the Bob Ross Floral Technique, but who also have our personal guarantee of excellence. These artists/instructors travel and teach on a contract basis and are also available for private or public demonstrations. You may contact the Bob Ross Company directly for their class schedules or you may prefer to ask your local art shop to arrange a class in your area.

WHAT INSTRUCTIONAL GUIDES ARE AVAILABLE?

Painting Packets (which include a color photo, complete instructions, basic technique and a line drawing) and videos, as well as book and videos by other artists, are available. These may be purchased from your local art shop or ordered directly from the Bob Ross Company.

HOW DO I BECOME AN INSTRUCTOR OF THIS TECHNIQUE?

To teach, you must be willing to devote the time necessary to master the technique and also be willing to share your knowledge and abilities with others. A love of people is an absolute necessity, as important as your ability to paint. Once these requirements are met, there is a program designed to teach and accredit individuals as Certified Ross Floral Instructors. Individuals who are accredited are very "special people" whom we have handpicked and trained to teach this technique of floral painting. More information is available upon request.

Look for the Complete Line of Bob Ross® Floral Painting Products

Visit your local art store
or call toll free
1-800-BOB-ROSS
(1-800-262-7677)

Bob Ross
Floral Painting Packets

Each beautiful painting packet includes a glossy color photo, complete written instructions and 18"x24" sketch for easy transfer to your canvas.

Collect them all!

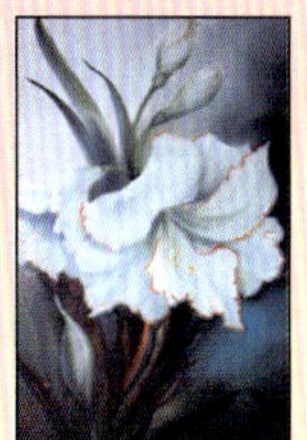
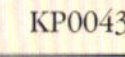
KP0043

KP001 Hibiscus Cluster
KP002 Fuchsias
KP003 Geraniums
KP004 Blue Morning Glories
KP005 English Shrub Roses
KP006 Pot o' Pink Poppies
KP007 Red and Pink Roses in Oval
KP008 Pastel Tulips
KP009 Pink Poppies
KP010 Bird of Paradise
KP011 Large Pansies
KP012 Cactus Flowers
KP013 Poinsettias
KP014 Pink Roses in Glass
KP015 Poppies in a Window
KP016 White Poppies
KP017 Basket of Tulips
KP018 Oval Pink Roses
KP019 "Peachy" Tulips
KP020 Basket of Sunflowers
KP021 Pot o' Poppies
KP022 Iris
KP023 Amaryllis
KP024 Calla Lilies
KP025 Pansies
KP026 Hollyhocks
KP027 Gladiolus
KP028 Sunflowers
KP029 Orchids
KP030 Red Hibiscus
KP031 Mums
KP036 White Lilies with Border
KP043 Bob Ross Amaryllis

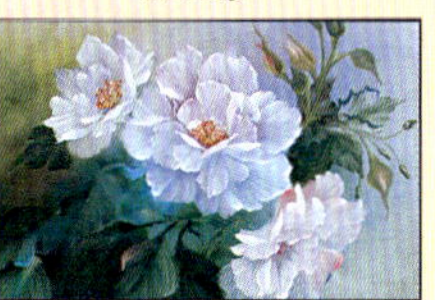
KP005

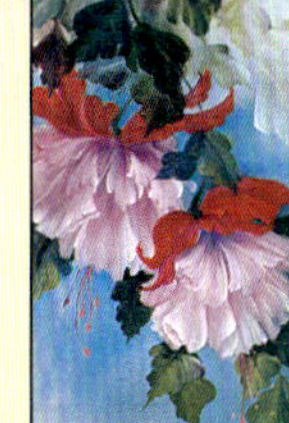
KP002

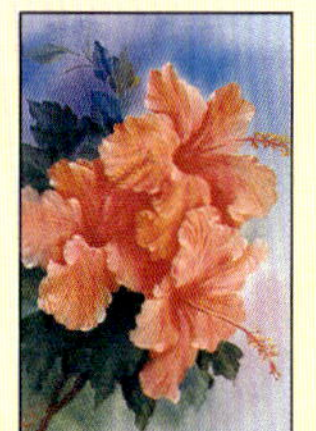
KP001

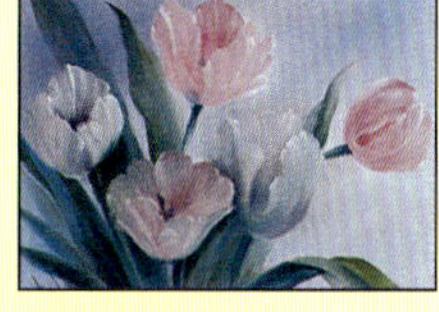
KP008

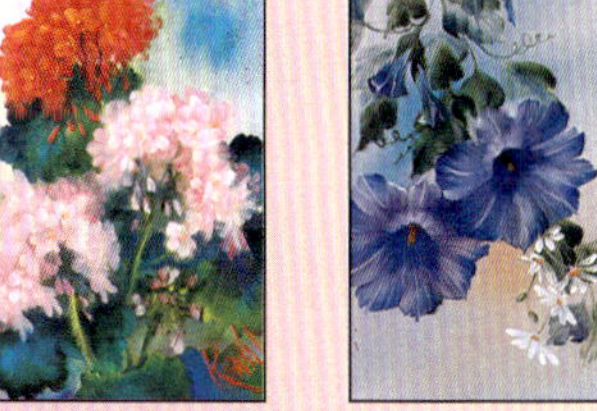
KP003

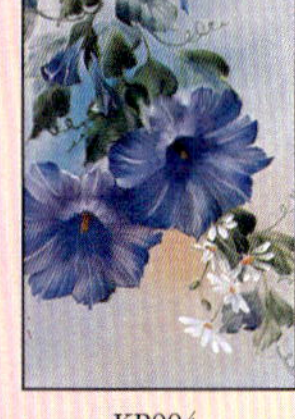
KP004

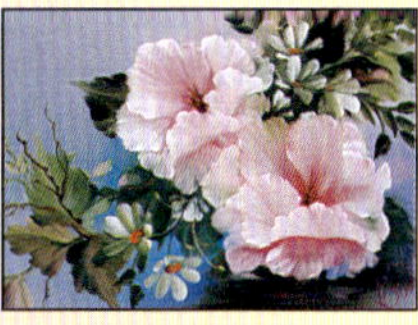
KP009

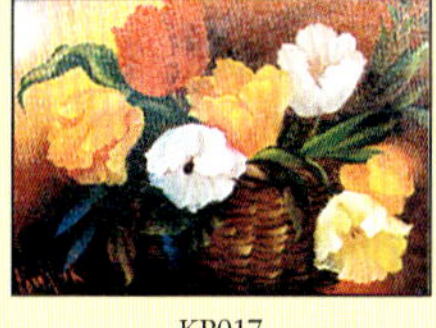
KP017

KP006 KP007 KP010 KP011 KP012

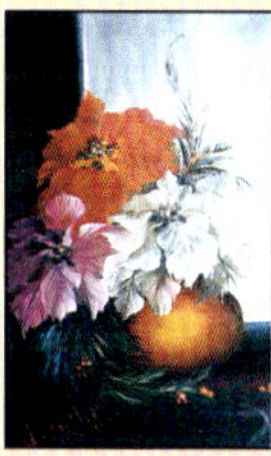
KP013

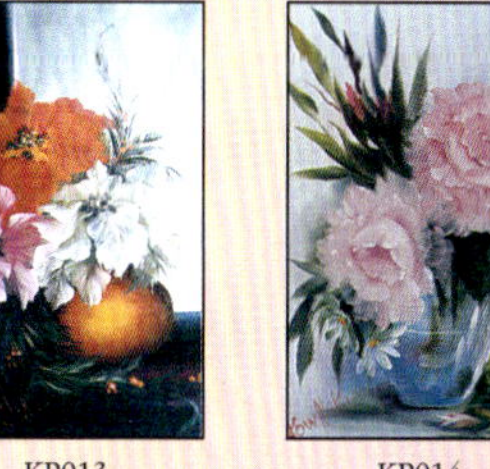
KP014

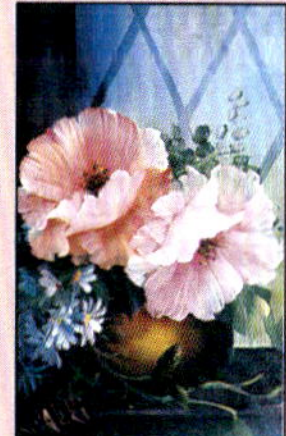
KP015

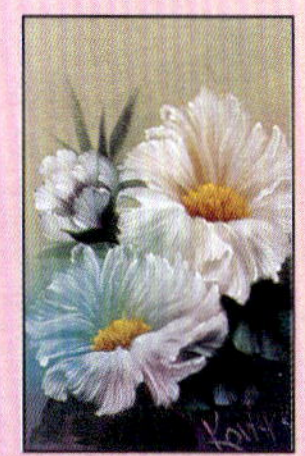
KP016

KP018 KP019 KP020 KP021 KP022 KP023 KP024

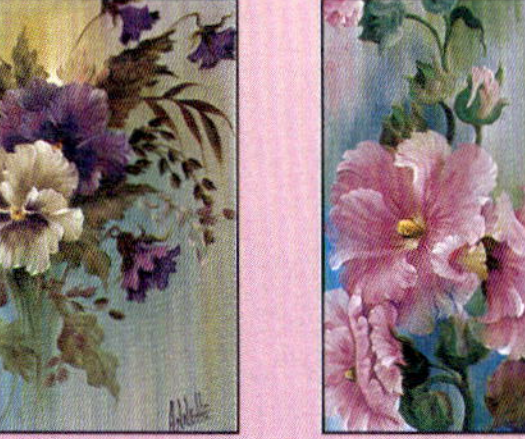
KP025

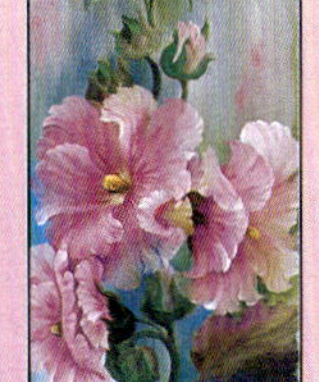
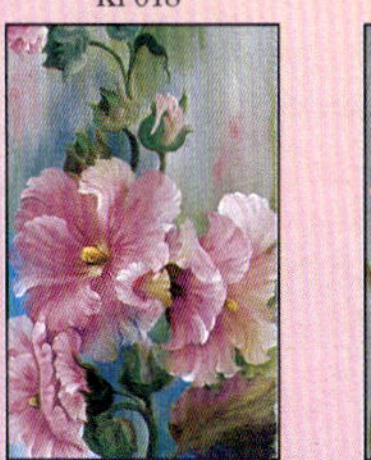
KP026

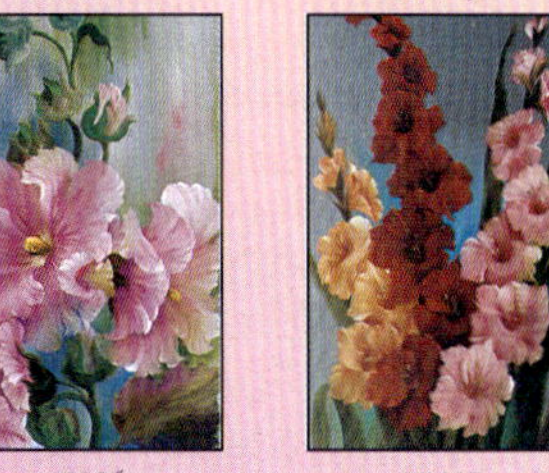
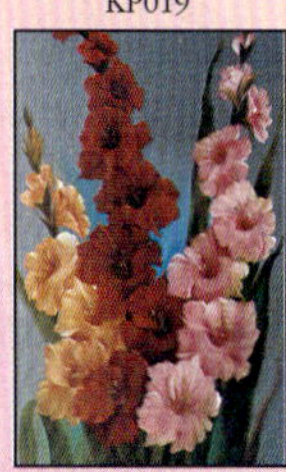
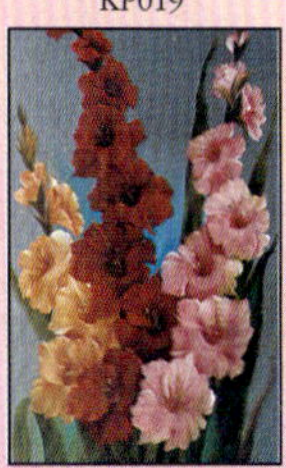
KP027

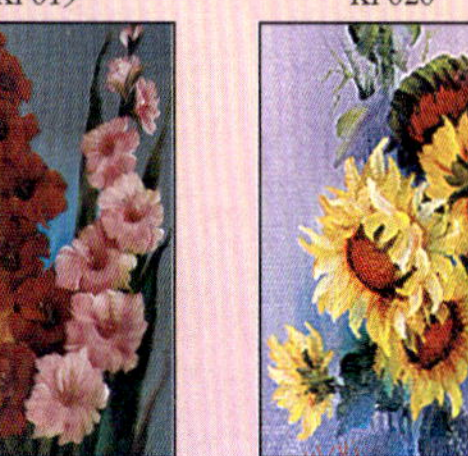
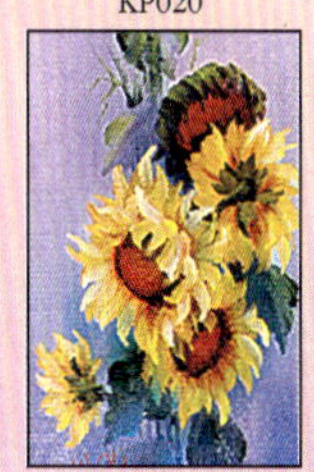
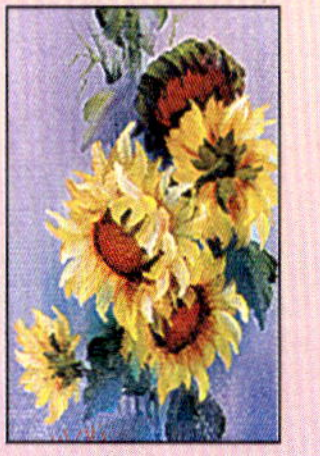
KP028

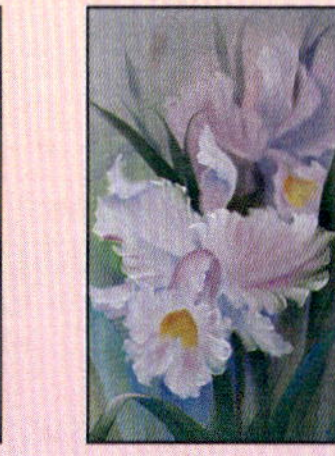
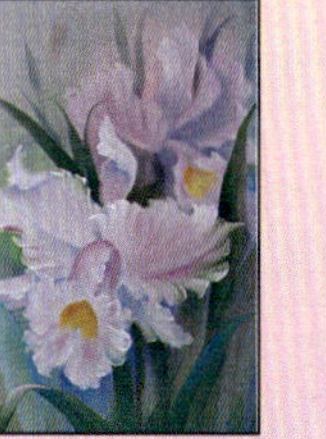
KP029

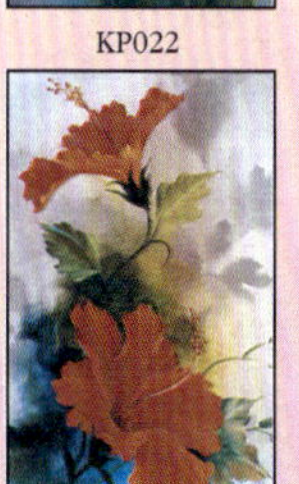
KP030

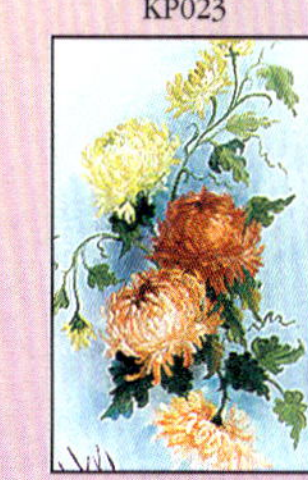
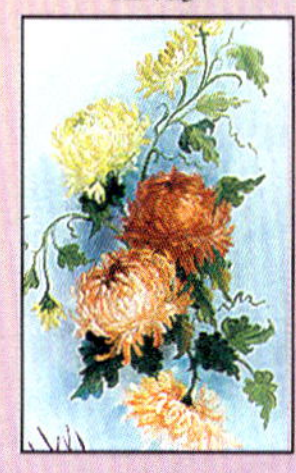
KP031

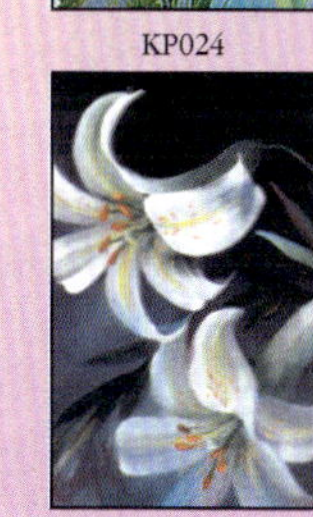
KP036

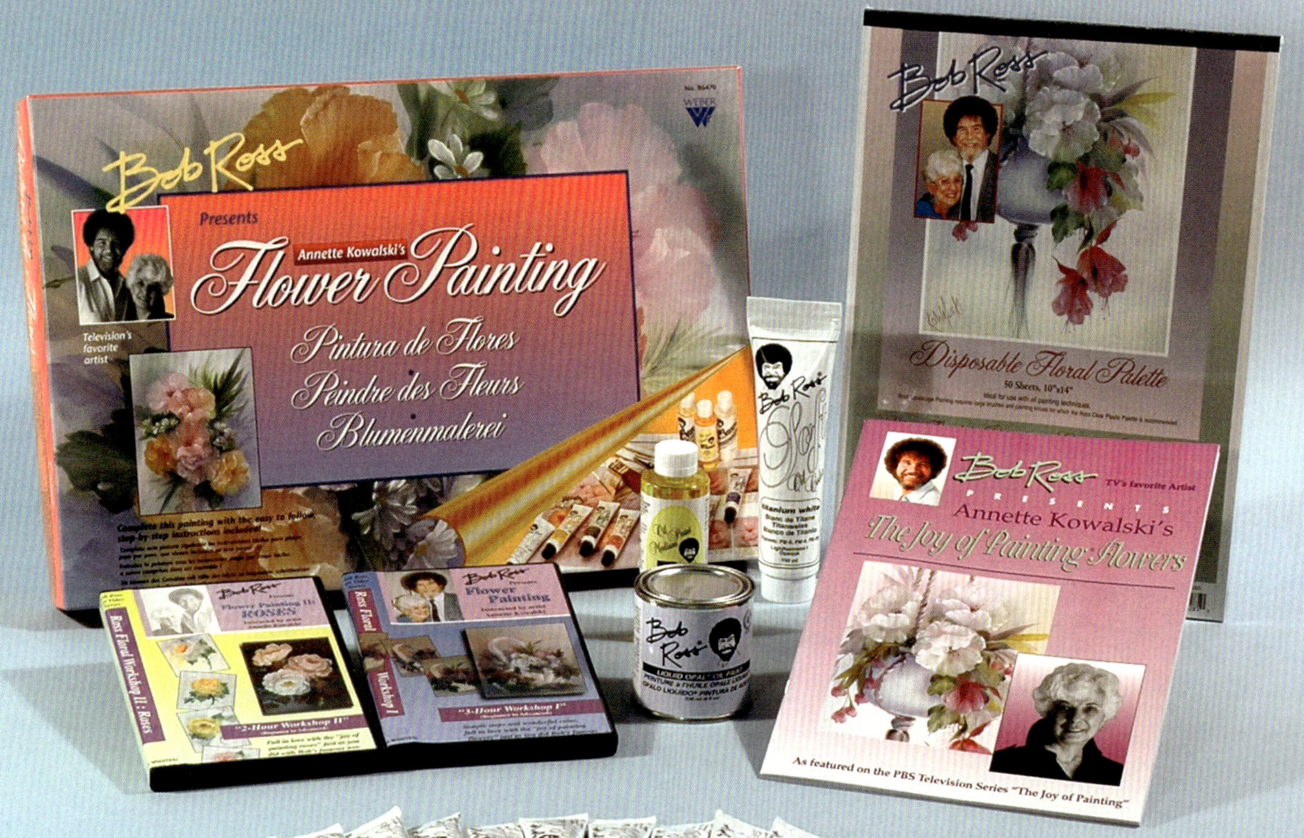

Bob Ross
Soft Oil Paints
Titanium White
Cadmium Yellow Light
Cadmium Orange
Flower Pink
Dusty Rose
Magenta
Cadmium Red Light
Cadmium Red Medium
Alizarin Crimson
Mauve
Ultramarine Blue
Turquoise
Sap Green
Viridian Green
Ivory Black

Bob Ross
Floral Brushes
2" Soft Blender Brush
1" Landscape Brush
3/4" Floral Brush
1/2" Floral Brush
Floral Filbert Brush
#4 Floral Fan Brush
Small Round Floral Brush
#2 Script Liner Brush

Bob Ross
Liquid Opal

Bob Ross
Oil Paint Medium

Bob Ross
Paper Palette

Bob Ross
Floral Books, Videos, DVDs
Joy of Painting Flowers I Book
Joy of Painting Flowers II Book
Joy of Painting Flowers Workshop I Video or DVD (3 hrs.)
Joy of Painting Flowers Workshop II "Roses" Video or DVD (2 hrs.)

Bob Ross Flower Painting Kit

Look for the Complete Line of
Bob Ross® Floral Painting
Products

Visit your local art store
or call toll free
1-800-BOB-ROSS
(1-800-262-7677)